SELECTED BY
PHYLLIS FREEMAN
MARK GREENBERG
ERIC HIMMEL
ANDREAS LANDSHOFF
CHARLES MIERS

HARRY N. ABRAMS, INC., PUBLISHERS, NEW YORK

NEW ART

DESIGNER: ELISSA ICHIYASU

LIBRARY OF CONGRESS CATALOGING-IN-PUBLICATION DATA
NEW ART/SELECTED BY PHYLLIS FREEMAN ... [ET AL.].
P.   CM.
ISBN 0-8109-2443-9
1. ART, MODERN—20TH CENTURY—THEMES, MOTIVES.
2. AVANT-GARDE (AESTHETICS)—HISTORY-20TH CENTURY—THEMES, MOTIVES.
I. FREEMAN, PHYLLIS.
N6493   1980.N48   1990   89-28322
709'.04—DC20   CIP

A TIMES MIRROR COMPANY
PRINTED AND BOUND IN JAPAN

IN 1984, WE PUBLISHED THE FIRST VOLUME OF *NEW ART,* SURVEYING ARTISTS WHO HAD ACHIEVED SOME DEGREE OF PROMINENCE IN THE UNITED STATES OVER THE PREVIOUS FIVE YEARS AND WHOSE WORK DEALT WITH ISSUES THAT WERE ENGAGING THE ART WORLD IN THE EARLY 1980S. FOR THIS VOLUME, COVERING THE MID-1980S TO 1990, OUR CRITERIA HAVE REMAINED THE SAME.

THE ART INCLUDED HERE IS AGAIN DIVERSE, CONFIRMING THAT MANY STYLES STILL COEXIST IN THE ART WORLD. WE NOTE AMONG RECENT TRENDS THE INCREASING PRESENCE OF WOMEN ARTISTS; THE REVIVAL OF INTEREST IN CONCEPTUAL ART AND GEOMETRIC ABSTRACTION; THE RENEWED VIGOR OF LANDSCAPE PAINTING AND POLITICAL ART; THE EMPLOYMENT BY ARTISTS AND GALLERIES OF INSTALLATION ALMOST AS A MEDIUM ITSELF; THE BROAD USE OF PHOTOGRAPHY AND COMPUTER-GENERATED IMAGERY, ON THE ONE HAND, AND NATURAL MATERIALS, ON THE OTHER; THE APPROPRIATION OF IMAGES FROM THE HISTORY OF ART AND POPULAR CULTURE; THE FABRICATION OF ENVIRONMENTS; AND THE ESTABLISHMENT OF A VIDEO FOOTHOLD IN TRADITIONAL GALLERIES.

IN THE END, ANY SELECTION SUCH AS THIS IS SUBJECTIVE. IN MAKING OURS, WE HAVE BEEN PAINFULLY AWARE THAT THERE ARE MORE GOOD LANDSCAPE PAINTERS OR GEOMETRIC ABSTRACTIONISTS, FOR EXAMPLE, THAN WE COULD INCLUDE IN THIS BOOK AND STILL HAVE ROOM TO SHOW A BROAD SPECTRUM OF WORK. WE HOPE, HOWEVER, THAT OUR CHOICES NOT ONLY ACCURATELY REPRESENT THE ART OF TODAY BUT WILL ALSO PROVOKE INTEREST IN THE WORK OF ARTISTS WHO HAVE ALREADY MADE THEIR MARK—AND FROM WHOM WE EXPECT TO HEAR AGAIN IN THE YEARS AHEAD.

WE WOULD LIKE TO THANK THE ARTISTS, GALLERIES, DEALERS, CURATORS, AND OTHERS WHO GENEROUSLY GAVE US THEIR SUGGESTIONS AS WELL AS THEIR TIME AND EFFORT IN PROCURING THE ILLUSTRATIONS FOR THIS BOOK. SPECIAL THANKS ALSO TO REBECCA TUCKER, CHRISTINE A. PIKE, AND VENETIA REECE OF HARRY N. ABRAMS, INC., FOR THEIR ASSISTANCE.

TERRY ALLEN

BORN: LUBBOCK, TEXAS

TERRY ALLEN
COVENANT, 1986
MIXED MEDIA, 81 × 60¾ × 36"
COURTESY JOHN WEBER GALLERY, NEW YORK

JOHN ARMLEDER

BORN: 1948, GENEVA, SWITZERLAND

JOHN ARMLEDER
UNTITLED FURNITURE SCULPTURE, 1988
ACRYLIC ON CANVAS WITH FOUR DINER STOOLS, 14 × 24'
PRIVATE COLLECTION
COURTESY JON GIBSON GALLERY, NEW YORK

DAVID BATES

BORN: 1952, DALLAS, TEXAS

DAVID BATES

WALLACE & CLOVIS, 1986
OIL ON CANVAS, 78 × 96"
COLLECTION EDWARD J. MINSKOFF
COURTESY CHARLES COWLES GALLERY, NEW YORK

DAVID BATES
PENNYWORT POOL, 1988
OIL ON CANVAS, 96 × 78"
PRIVATE COLLECTION
COURTESY CHARLES COWLES GALLERY, NEW YORK

TONY BEVAN

BORN: 1951, BRADFORD, ENGLAND

TONY BEVAN
EXPOSED ARM, 1987
PIGMENT AND ACRYLIC ON CANVAS, 53½ × 41"
COURTESY LOUVER GALLERY, NEW YORK

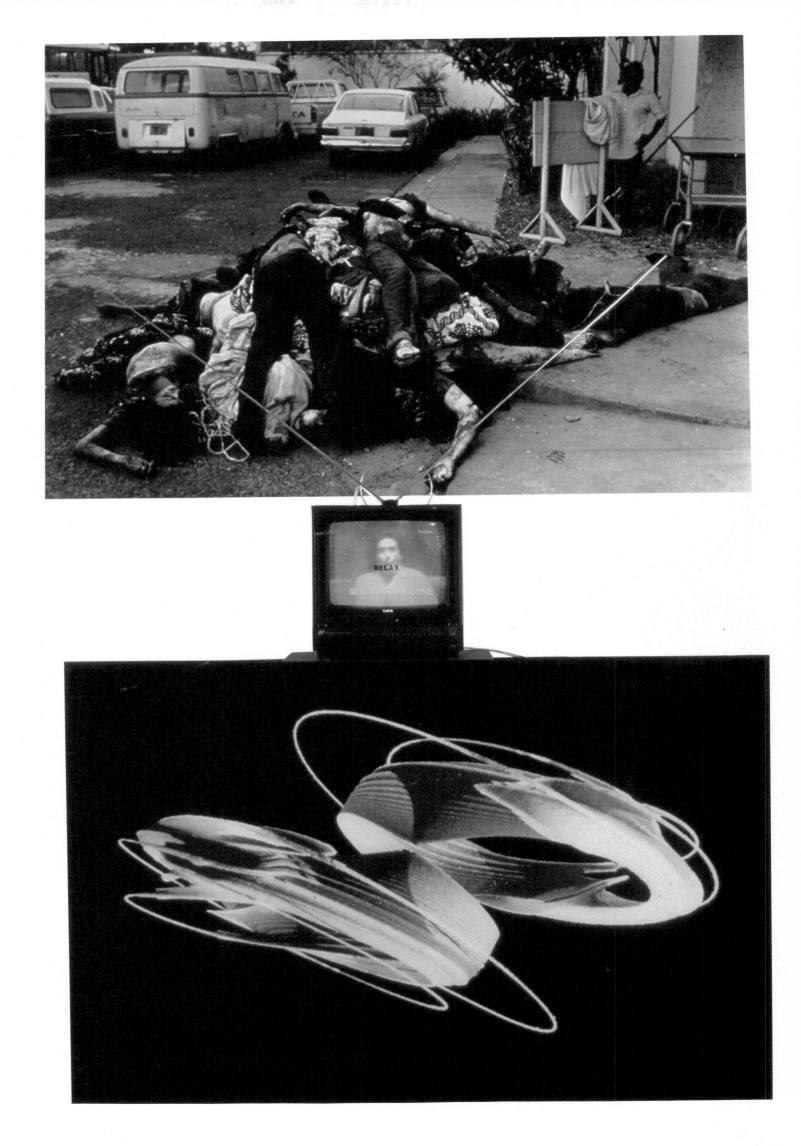

GRETCHEN BENDER

UNTITLED (RELAX), 1988
TV, SILKSCREEN ON ACETATE, LAMINATED COLOR,
BLACK-AND-WHITE PHOTOS, METAL SHELF, 113 × 72 × 15"
COURTESY METRO PICTURES, NEW YORK

GRETCHEN BENDER

BORN: 1951, SEAFORD, DELAWARE

GRETCHEN BENDER
UNTITLED (FROM *THE PLEASURE IS BACK* SERIES), 1981–82
SILKSCREENED TIN, 72 × 72"
EDITION OF 6
COURTESY METRO PICTURES, NEW YORK

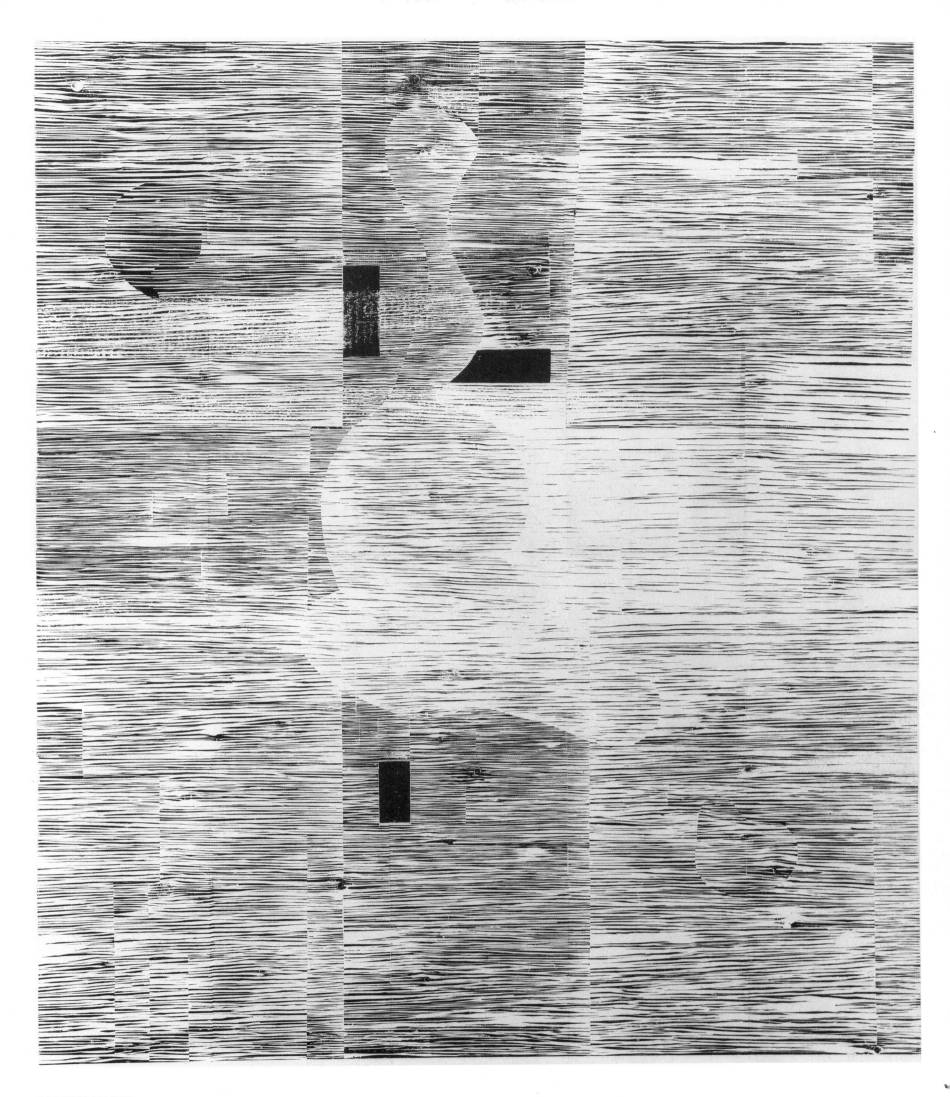

DOMENICO BIANCHI
UNTITLED, 1989
XYLOGRAPH ON PAPER, 79½ × 79¾"
COURTESY SPERONE WESTWATER GALLERY, NEW YORK

DOMENICO BIANCHI

BORN: 1955, ROME, ITALY

15

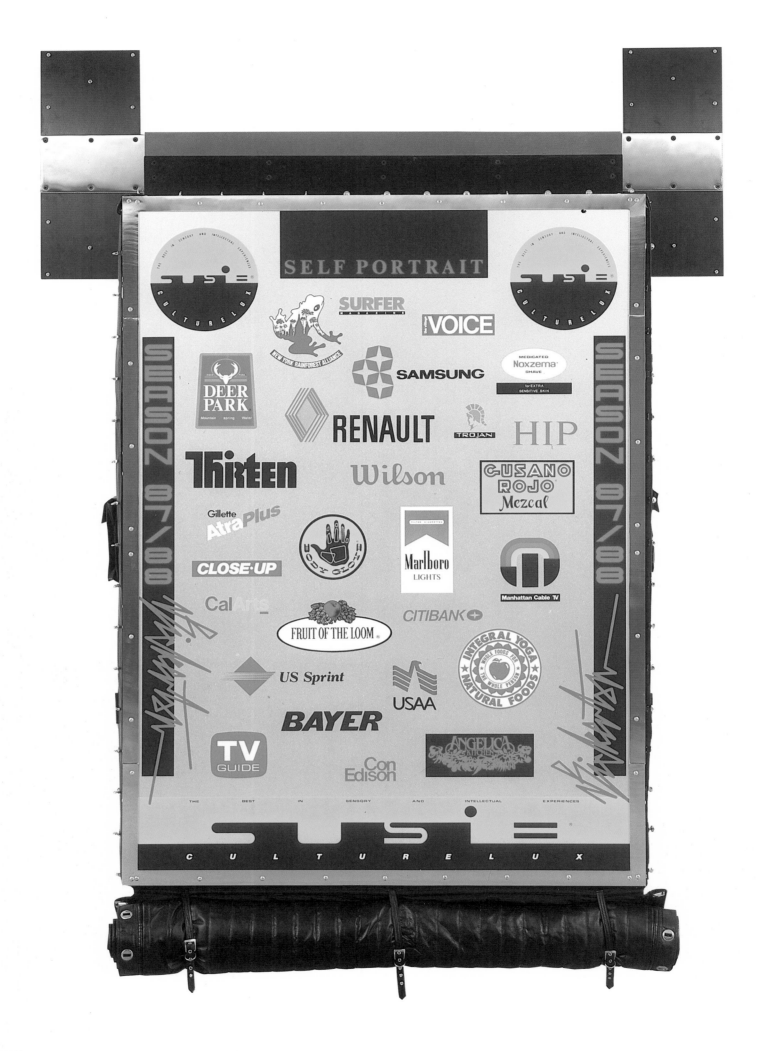

ASHLEY BICKERTON
TORMENTED SELF-PORTRAIT, 1988
MIXED-MEDIA CONSTRUCTION WITH BLACK PADDED LEATHER, 90 × 69 × 18"
COURTESY SONNABEND GALLERY, NEW YORK

ASHLEY BICKERTON

BORN: 1959, BARBADOS

ASHLEY BICKERTON
INTERIOR (WICKED TAHITI), 1988
MIXED-MEDIA CONSTRUCTION, 96 × 258¼ × 26½"
COURTESY SONNABEND GALLERY, NEW YORK

ROSS BLECKNER

BORN: 1949, NEW YORK CITY

ROSS BLECKNER
ARCHITECTURE OF THE SKY I, 1988
OIL ON CANVAS, 106 × 92"
COURTESY MARY BOONE GALLERY, NEW YORK

ROSS BLECKNER
THE THIRD EXAMINED LIFE, 1988. OIL ON LINEN, 96 × 72"
COLLECTION VIJAK MAHDAVI AND BERNARDO NADAL-GINARD, BOSTON
COURTESY MARY BOONE GALLERY, NEW YORK

MIKE BIDLO

BORN: 1953, CHICAGO, ILLINOIS

MIKE BIDLO
NOT WARHOL (BONWIT TELLER, 1961), 1989
INSTALLATION, GREY ART GALLERY WINDOW
COURTESY THE ARTIST

MIKE BIDLO
PICASSO'S WOMEN, 1988
STUDIO VIEW OF WORKS EXHIBITED AT THE LEO CASTELLI GALLERY
COURTESY THE ARTIST

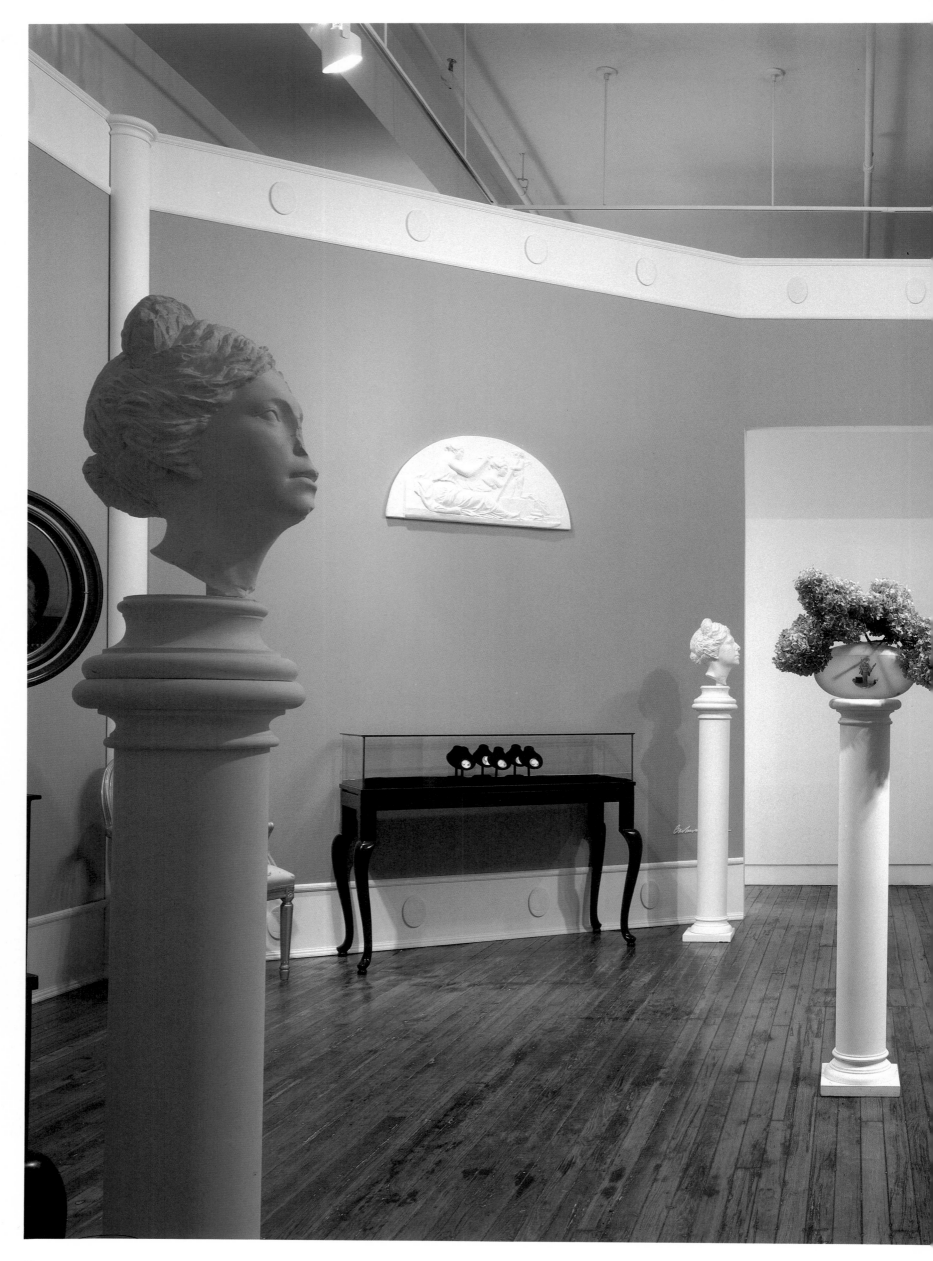

BARBARA BLOOM
REIGN OF NARCISSISM, 1989
INSTALLATION AT JAY GORNEY MODERN ART,
NEW YORK, SEPTEMBER 1989
COURTESY JAY GORNEY MODERN ART, NEW YORK

JENNIFER BOLANDE

BORN: 1957, CLEVELAND, OHIO

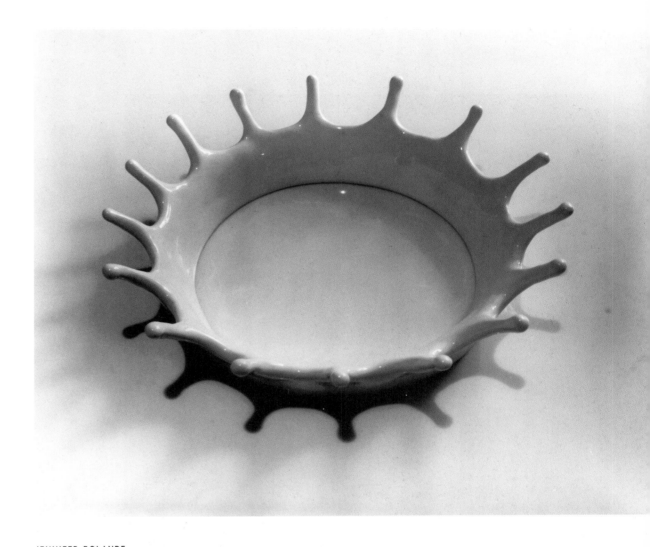

JENNIFER BOLANDE

MILK CROWN, 1987–88
CAST PORCELAIN, 2 × 7"
EDITION OF 6
COURTESY METRO PICTURES, NEW YORK

JENNIFER BOLANDE

CASCADING PHOTOGRAPH, 1987
PHOTOGRAPH, 144 × 36"
COURTESY METRO PICTURES, NEW YORK

ELLEN BROOKS

BORN: LOS ANGELES, CALIFORNIA

ELLEN BROOKS
UNTITLED (GARDEN SLICE), 1987
CIBACHROME PRINT, 89 × 46"
COURTESY ANNINA NOSEI GALLERY, NEW YORK

ELLEN BROOKS
UNTITLED (DAYLIGHT TREES), 1987
CIBACHROME PRINT, 42½ × 157"
COURTESY ANNINA NOSEI GALLERY, NEW YORK

 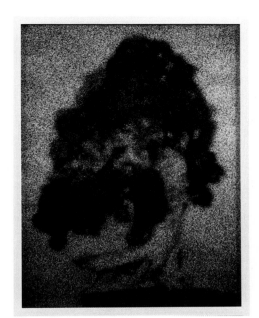 

NANCY BURSON

BORN: 1948, ST. LOUIS, MISSOURI

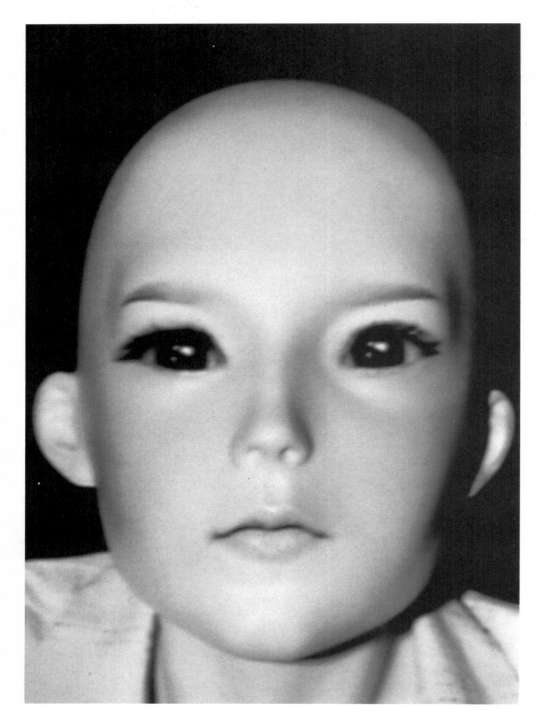

NANCY BURSON
UNTITLED, 1988
POLAROID POLACOLOR ER PRINT, 24 × 20"
COURTESY JAYNE H. BAUM GALLERY, NEW YORK

COLIN CHASE
SPIRIT CATCHER # 9, 1989
MIXED MEDIA, WOOD, AND STEEL, 99 × 62 × 18"
COLLECTION THE ARTIST
COURTESY JUNE KELLY GALLERY, NEW YORK

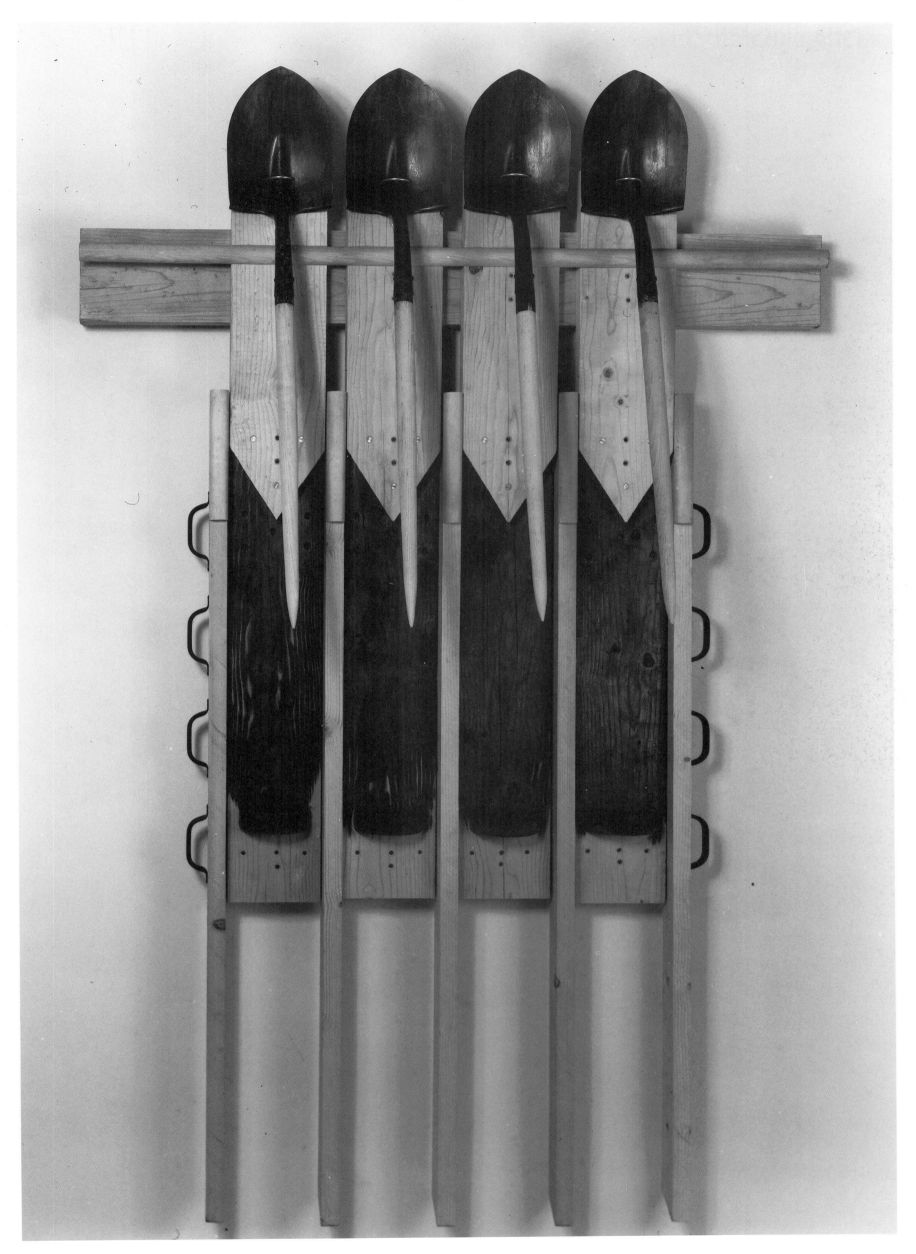

GRISHA BRUSKIN

BORN: 1945, MOSCOW, U.S.S.R.

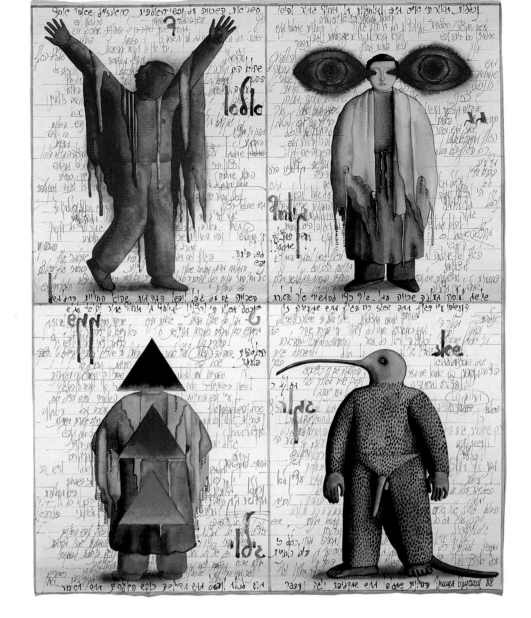

GRISHA BRUSKIN
UNTITLED, 1988
GOUACHE, 22 × 17"
COURTESY MARLBOROUGH GALLERY, NEW YORK

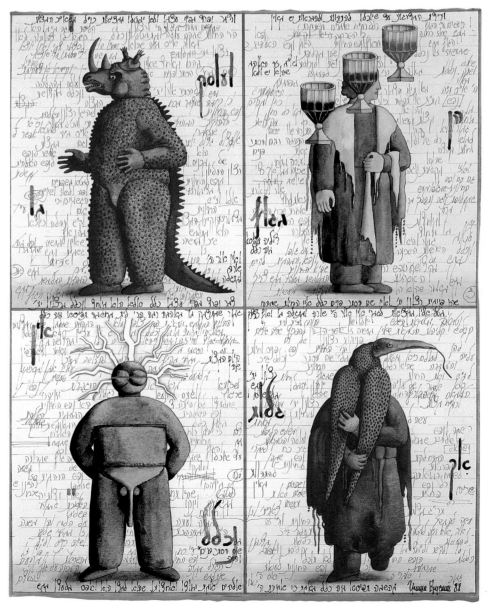

GRISHA BRUSKIN
UNTITLED, 1988
GOUACHE, 22 × 17"
COURTESY MARLBOROUGH GALLERY, NEW YORK

GRISHA BRUSKIN

UNTITLED, 1989
OIL ON CANVAS, 47 × 36"
COURTESY MARLBOROUGH GALLERY, NEW YORK

JAMES CASEBERE

BORN: 1953, LANSING, MICHIGAN

JAMES CASEBERE

WESTERN SCULPTURE WITH TWO WAGONS AND CANNON, 1987
STYROFOAM, WOOD, EPOXY, FIBERGLASS, AND PAINT
INSTALLATION AT WALKER ART CENTER
COURTESY MICHAEL KLEIN, INC., NEW YORK

JAMES CASEBERE
CHUCKWAGON WITH YUCCA, 1988
SILVERPRINT, 40 × 50"
COURTESY MICHAEL KLEIN, INC., NEW YORK

SAINT CLAIR CEMIN

BORN: 1951, CUZA ALTA, BRAZIL

SAINT CLAIR CEMIN

UNTITLED, 1988
MAHOGANY AND BRONZE, UNIQUE, 14½ × 43 × 14½"
COURTESY MASSIMO AUDIELLO GALLERY, NEW YORK

SAINT CLAIR CEMIN
UNTITLED (LARGE TABLE), 1988
BRONZE, TERRA-COTTA, AND MARBLE, 5 × 8 × 2½'
COURTESY MASSIMO AUDIELLO GALLERY, NEW YORK

CHING HO CHENG

BORN: 1946, HAVANA, CUBA
DIED: 1989, NEW YORK CITY

CHING HO CHENG
INSTALLATION AT THE GREY ART GALLERY, 1987–88
IRON OXIDE ON PAPER, 10'9" × 28'8"
COURTESY SYBAO CHENG-WILSON, NEW YORK

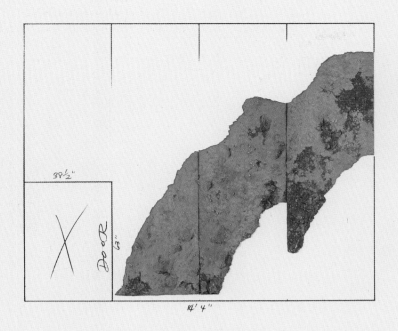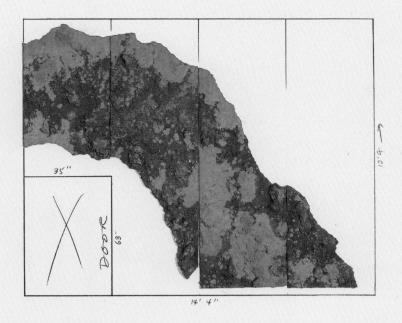

SUE COE

WHEEL OF FORTUNE....TODAY'S PIG IS TOMORROW'S BACON, 1989
WATERCOLOR, GOUACHE, COLLAGE, GRAPHITE, ACRYLIC, AND REMBRANDT
BLACK PRINTER'S INK ON WHITE STRATHMORE BRISTOL PAPER, 58⅜ × 55⅝"
COURTESY GALERIE ST. ETIENNE, NEW YORK
COPYRIGHT © 1989, SUE COE

SUE COE

COLD CUTS, 1989
WATERCOLOR, GRAPHITE, AND REMBRANDT BLACK PRINTER'S INK
ON WHITE STRATHMORE BRISTOL PAPER, 57 × 40"
COURTESY GALERIE ST. ETIENNE, NEW YORK
COPYRIGHT © 1989, SUE COE

STEVE DIBENEDETTO

BORN: 1958, BRONX, NEW YORK

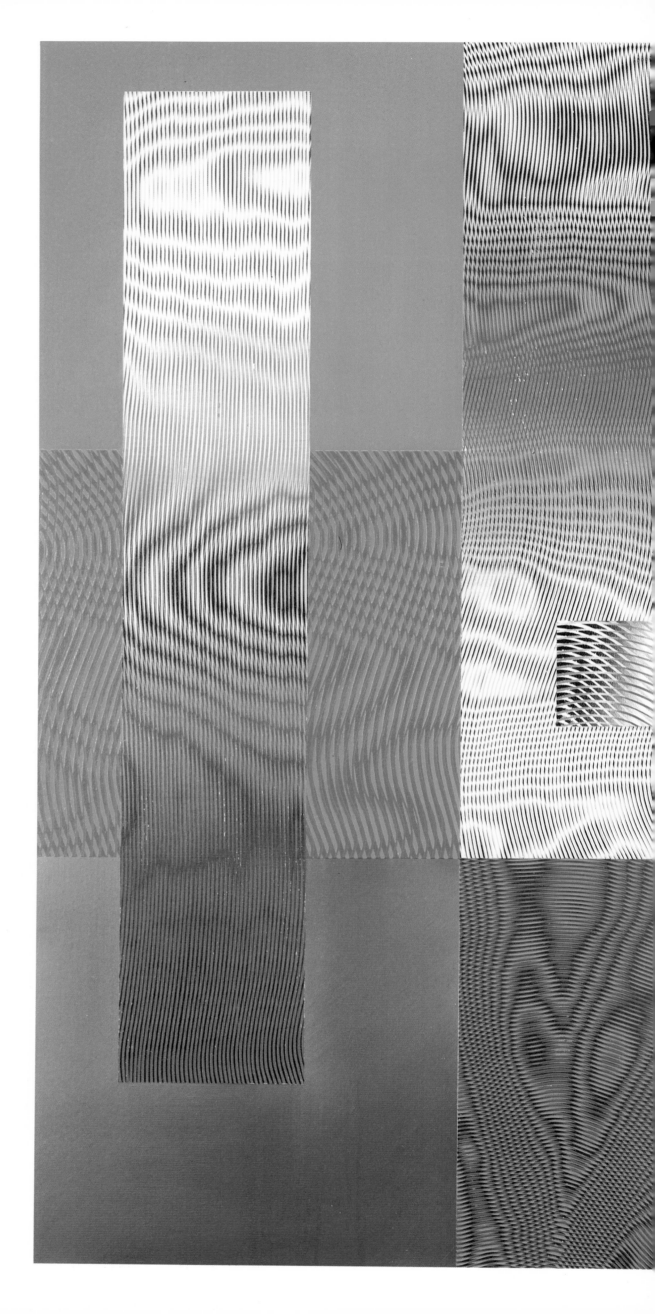

STEVE DIBENEDETTO
SCENE MISSING (FOR D.H.), 1988
ACRYLIC ON CANVAS, 60 × 60"
COURTESY CLARISSA DALRYMPLE

KATHERINE DOYLE
THE CHESAPEAKE, 1989
OIL ON CANVAS, 36 × 60"
COURTESY SCHMIDT BINGHAM GALLERY, NEW YORK

KATHERINE DOYLE
THE CHESAPEAKE AT DUSK, 1987
OIL ON CANVAS, 36 × 60"
THE SEAVAST COLLECTION, NEW YORK
COURTESY SCHMIDT BINGHAM GALLERY, NEW YORK

JANE DICKSON
PIERROT, 1987
OIL ON CANVAS, 48 × 104"
COURTESY BROOKE ALEXANDER GALLERY, NEW YORK

JANE DICKSON

BORN: 1952, CHICAGO, ILLINOIS

DEBBY DAVIS

BORN: 1949, HARTFORD, CONNECTICUT

DEBBY DAVIS
TWO WHITE PIGEONS, 1988
LAMINATED CIBACHROME PRINT, 30 × 30"
COURTESY ELIZABETH MCDONALD GALLERY, NEW YORK

ORSHI DROZDIK

ETHER ANAESTHESIA, 1988
METAL, PORCELAIN, PLASTIC TUBING, LEAD, GLASS BOTTLE,
STEEL, AND GLASS, 34½ × 25 × 13¼"
COURTESY TOM CUGLIANI GALLERY, NEW YORK

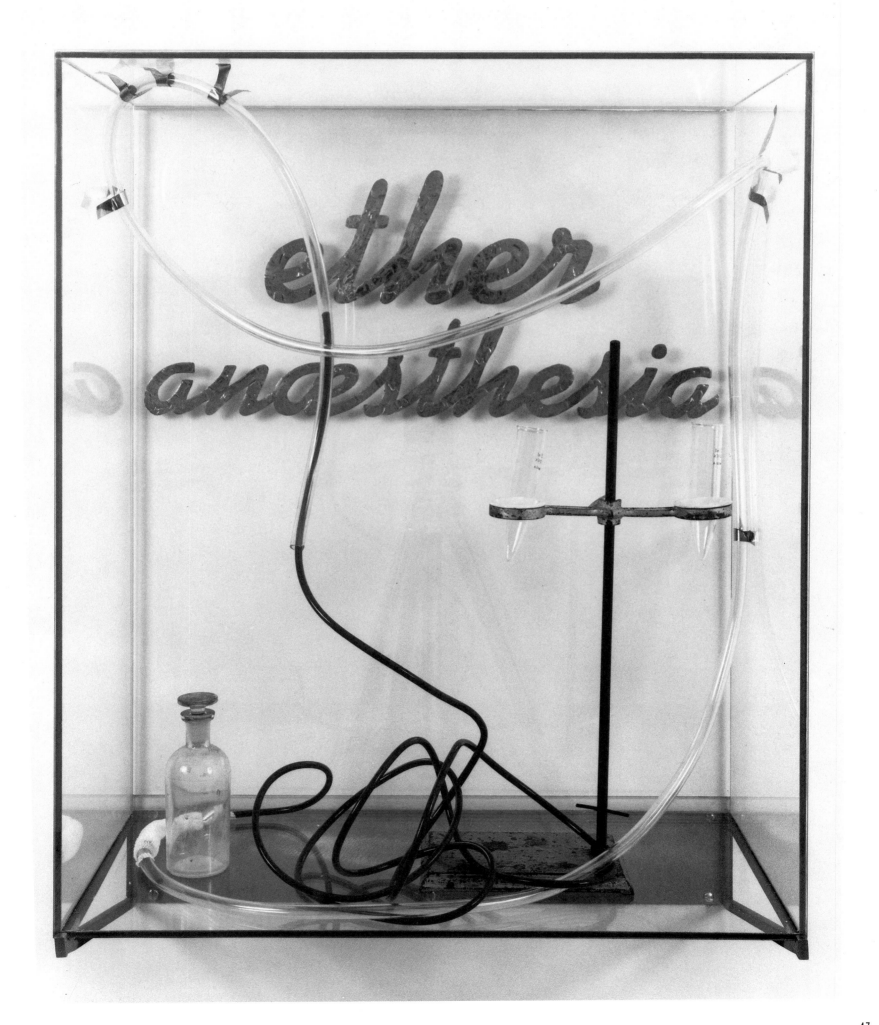

RANDY DUDLEY

BORN: 1950, PEORIA, ILLINOIS

RANDY DUDLEY
GOWANUS CANAL FROM BOND STREET, 1987
OIL ON CANVAS, 28½ × 54"
COURTESY OK HARRIS WORKS OF ART, NEW YORK

CAROLINA ESCOBAR

BORN: 1951, MINNESOTA

CAROLINA ESCOBAR
MARCH, 1989
HYDROSTONE AND LEAD, 6 × 5 × 10'
COURTESY MICHAEL INGBAR GALLERY, NEW YORK

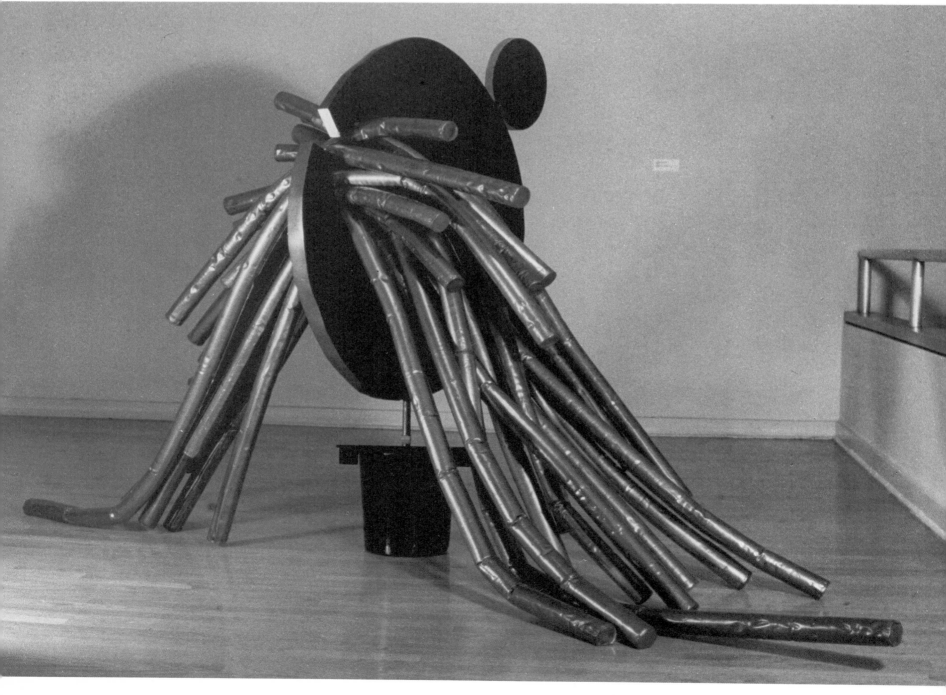

BARBARA ESS

UNTITLED, 1986–88
MONOCHROME COLOR PHOTOGRAPH, 30 × 40"
COURTESY CURT MARCUS GALLERY, NEW YORK

CHRISTIAN ECKART

AFTER MALEVICH (REIFIED ACCORDINGLY), 1986
LEFT: GOLD LEAF ON WOOD WITH PLEXIGLAS;
RIGHT: ALUMINUM LEAF ON WOOD WITH PLEXIGLAS,
EACH 32 × 32"
COURTESY MASSIMO AUDIELLO GALLERY, NEW YORK

CHRISTIAN ECKART

BORN: 1958, CALGARY, CANADA

CHRISTIAN ECKART
WHITE PAINTING (#102), 1987
FORMICA SEVEN AND 22-CARAT GOLD LEAF ON WOOD, 96½ × 84½"
COURTESY MASSIMO AUDIELLO GALLERY, NEW YORK

R. M. FISCHER

BORN: 1947, NEW YORK CITY

R. M. FISCHER

RECTOR GATE, 1985–89
BATTERY PARK CITY, NEW YORK
COURTESY THE ARTIST

R. M. FISCHER

STATIONS, 1987
INSTALLATION, BASKERVILLE & WATSON GALLERY, NEW YORK
STAINLESS STEEL, ALUMINUM, AND BRASS
COLLECTION ROBERT SHIFFLER
COURTESY THE ARTIST

HELMUT FEDERLE
*ULAN BATOR (BASICS ON COMPOSITION;
DIAGONAL),* 1987
ACRYLIC ON LINEN, 94½ × 136"
COURTESY MARY BOONE GALLERY, NEW YORK

JOEL FISHER

PEGASUS, 1987
BRONZE, EDITION OF THREE, 12¾ × 2¾ × 13¾"
COURTESY DIANE BROWN GALLERY, NEW YORK

HELMUT FEDERLE

UNRUHIGES BILD MIT EINSEITIGEM GEWICHT, 1986
OIL ON LINEN, 110 × 74¾"
COLLECTION DON AND DORIS FISHER, SAN FRANCISCO
COURTESY MARY BOONE GALLERY, NEW YORK

STEPHEN FRAILEY

BORN: 1957, EVANSTON, ILLINOIS

JILL GIEGERICH

UNTITLED, 1988
RUBBER, XEROX, SHELLAC WITH PIGMENT, CHARCOAL,
AND PAINT-STICK ON GESSOED PLYWOOD, 91¼ × 70¼"
THE ELI BROAD FAMILY FOUNDATION, LOS ANGELES
COURTESY MARGO LEAVIN GALLERY, LOS ANGELES

JILL GIEGERICH
UNTITLED, 1986
VINYL, COPPER, INK PRINT COLLAGE ON PAPER
MOUNTED ON PLYWOOD, 106 × 73 × 4"
COLLECTION NEWPORT HARBOR ART MUSEUM;
PURCHASED WITH FUNDS PROVIDED BY THE AWARDS IN THE VISUAL ARTS
(A PROGRAM SPONSORED BY THE EQUITABLE FOUNDATION AND
THE ROCKEFELLER FOUNDATION) AND BY THE ACQUISITIONS COMMITTEE

JILL GIEGERICH
UNTITLED, 1987
RUBBER, WOOD PRINT COLLAGE ON PAPER, GESSO, CHARCOAL, TRACING PAPER,
AND ASPHALT EMULSION ON PLYWOOD, 70¼ × 53½ × 2¾"
CITY OF SEATTLE ONE % FOR ART,
SEATTLE CITY LIGHT COLLECTION
COURTESY MARGO LEAVIN GALLERY, LOS ANGELES

ROBERT GINDER

2213, 1987
OIL AND GOLD LEAF ON WOOD, 36 × 48"
COURTESY OK HARRIS WORKS OF ART, NEW YORK

ROBERT GINDER
ONE WITH, 1987
OIL AND GOLD LEAF ON WOOD, 40 × 54″
COURTESY OK HARRIS WORKS OF ART, NEW YORK

ROBERT GOBER

BORN: 1954, WALLINGFORD, CONNECTICUT

ROBERT GOBER

UNTITLED DOOR AND DOORFRAME, 1987–88
WOOD, ENAMEL PAINT, DOOR, 84 × 34 × 1½"
FRAME: 90 × 43 × 5½"
COURTESY PAULA COOPER GALLERY, NEW YORK

ROBERT GOBER

UNTITLED, 1988
WOOD, ENAMEL, AND PAINT, 32 × 33 × 24"
COURTESY PAULA COOPER GALLERY, NEW YORK

ANTONY GORMLEY

THREE CALLS (PLUMB, CAST, AND PASS), 1983–84
LEAD, FIBERGLASS, AND PLASTER, 40 × 40 × 72"
COLLECTION OF ANNE AND MARTIN Z. MARGULIES, MIAMI, FLORIDA
COURTESY SALVATORE ALA GALLERY, NEW YORK

ANTONY GORMLEY

BORN: 1950, LONDON, ENGLAND

ANTONY GORMLEY
FATHERS AND SONS, 1985–86
LEAD, FIBERGLASS, AND PLASTER,
LEFT: 101½ × 26¾ × 20"; RIGHT: 26½ × 9½ × 8½"
COLLECTION OF THE METRO COMPANIES,
CRESCENT CENTER, ATLANTA, GEORGIA
COURTESY SALVATORE ALA GALLERY, NEW YORK

ANTONY GORMLEY
MAN ASLEEP, 1985
LEAD, FIBERGLASS, PLASTER, AND TERRA-COTTA
COURTESY SALVATORE ALA, NEW YORK

GROUP MATERIAL
POLITICS AND ELECTIONS
INSTALLATION AT DIA ART FOUNDATION, NEW YORK, 1988
COURTESY DIA ART FOUNDATION, NEW YORK

RENT

CONTROL

GROUP MATERIAL

FOUNDED: 1979
DOUGLAS ASHFORD
BORN: 1958, MOROCCO
JULIE AULT
BORN: 1957, MASSACHUSETTS
FELIX GONZALEZ-TORRES
BORN: 1957, CUBA
KAREN RAMSPACHER
BORN: 1965: PENNSYLVANIA

GROUP MATERIAL

INSERTS
ADVERTISING SUPPLEMENT TO
THE NEW YORK *TIMES*, MAY 22, 1988
SPONSORED BY THE PUBLIC ART FUND, INC.,
WITH THE NEW YORK STATE COUNCIL ON
THE ARTS AND ART MATTERS, INC.

INSERTS

A project by Group Material with artworks (front to back) by: Mike Glier, Jenny Holzer, Barbara Kruger, Carrie Mae Weems, Felix Gonzalez-Torres, Nancy Spero, Nancy Linn, Hans Haacke, Richard Prince, Louise Lawler. This project was organized by Doug Ashford, Julie Ault, and Felix Gonzalez-Torres for Group Material.

● Public Art Fund Inc.
25 Central Park West
Suite 25F
New York, New York
10023
▲ (212) 541-8423

Inserts is sponsored by the Public Art Fund Inc. with the generous support of the New York State Council on the Arts, and Art Matters, Inc.

Artworks courtesy of the artists and Barbara Gladstone Gallery, Mary Boone Gallery, Josh Baer Gallery, John Weber Gallery, and Metro Pictures.

© Group Material

ADVERTISING SUPPLEMENT

GROUP MATERIAL

Advertising Supplement to
The New York Times

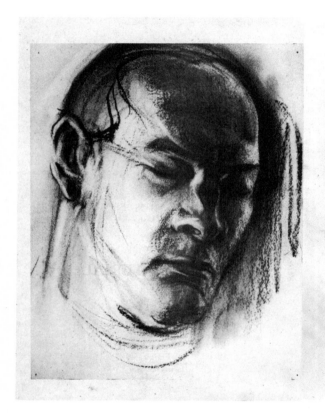

I AM A MAN.
I ENTER SPACE BECAUSE
IT EMPTIES ME.
I CHASE PEOPLE
AROUND THE HOUSE.
I SLEEP ON MY BACK
FOR SIGHTS OF SEX
THAT MAKES BLOOD.
I PROTECT WHAT MULTIPLIES
BUT I AM NOT CERTAIN
THAT I LOVE MY BOY.
THERE IS PLEASURE
IN STOPPING MY FLESH
WHEN IT DOES WRONG.
GETTING WHAT I WANT
MAKES ME SICK.
WHY I FIGHT IS
NOT YOUR BUSINESS.
I LIKE DYING AND I AM SURE
I CAN DO IT MORE THAN ONCE.
I NEED PERFECTION BUT
WHEN I IMPLEMENT IT
HALF OF EVERYONE DIES.
I HAVE A LOT OF ACCIDENTS
AND I THINK THEY ARE FUNNY.
I EMPLOY PEOPLE TO MAKE
MY HOURS LIKE DREAMS.
I LIKE A CIRCLE OF
BODIES WHOSE HANDS
DO WHAT THEY SHOULD.
I WILL KILL YOU FOR
WHAT YOU MIGHT DO.

We don't need another hero

Peaches

Elaine

Tanikka

Liz

No, really. I am shocked. I mean the images of Black women are just down right strange. In some cases the images are so monstrously ugly that they scared me! Indeed, if I were as ugly as American culture has made me out to be. I'd hide my head like an ostrich in the sand, burying it so long, when I pulled it out, I'd have the look of a thousand-year-old egg. All marble and nerve. In some cases, like that pickaninny or beautiful African queen mess, these images are so unlike me—my sisters or any other women I know—I didn't know it was supposed to be me. No, really. In history, in media, in photographs, in literature, the construction of Black women as the embodiment of difference is so deep, so wide, so vast, so completely absorbed of reality that I didn't know it was me being made fun of, somebody had to tell me. Images so strangely funny one had to laugh. Laugh hard, long, loud. Had to. No, really. To lift the voice in laughter is saying something, I don't always know exactly what, but saying something nonetheless. We don't laugh to keep from crying, we laugh to keep from slapping the inventor of these crazy-ass-images upside his head, 'cause you can bet they re made by men. And though not completely voiceless in her construction—even the hands of women are dirty—these images like a noose about the neck, dangle from thin threads of desire wrapped around fingers owned by men, some White, some Black. No, really.

Poland 1939 Pearl Harbor 1941 Nuremberg 1946 Ike 1952 Geneva 1955 LBJ 1964 Bruce Lee 1973

In Memoriam

A YOUNG MOTHER DIED OF AIDS OCTOBER 7, 1987.

© NANCY LINN

THE DEPARTMENT OF HEALTH   AIDS INFORMATION   718 485-8111

REAGAN'S FREEDOM FIGHTERS WERE HERE

Arturo Robles, the photographer of this picture, wrote to JB Pictures, his New York photo agency: ''I am sending you, enclosed herewith, a pack of ten rolls:

· Photos of 4 dead contras, shot in the streets.
· Photos of 9 corpses of Sandinista soldiers and 4 civilians who died during the fire fight. These corpses are in coffins.
· Relatives of the dead carrying a cross, flowers, and a coffin.

The clash occurred in San José de Bocay on June 16, lasting for about 6 hours. The total number of dead was twenty-five: 12 contras, 9 Sandinista soldiers, 7 civilians.''

FIREMAN PULLING DRUNK OUT OF A BURNING BED: "YOU DARNED FOOL, THAT'LL TEACH YOU TO SMOKE IN BED." DRUNK: "I WASN'T SMOKING IN BED, IT WAS ON FIRE WHEN I laid down."

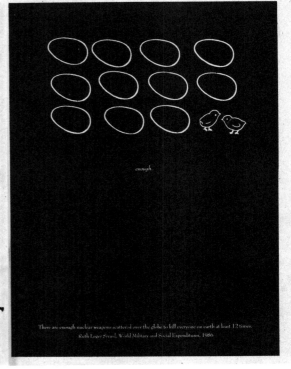

enough.

There are enough nuclear weapons scattered over the globe to kill everyone on earth at least 12 times.
Ruth Leger Sivard, World Military and Social Expenditures, 1986

PETER HALLEY
CELL WITH SMOKESTACK, 1987
ACRYLIC AND DAY-GLO ACRYLIC, ROLL-A-TEX ON CANVAS, 82¾ × 123½"
COURTESY SONNABEND GALLERY, NEW YORK

PETER HALLEY

BORN: 1953, NEW YORK CITY

PETER HALLEY
RED CELL, 1988–89
ACRYLIC AND ROLL-A-TEX ON CANVAS, 87 × 102"
COURTESY SONNABEND GALLERY, NEW YORK

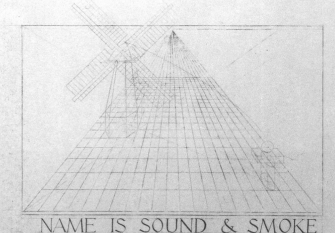

NAME IS SOUND & SMOKE

LES · MALHEURS · DE · LA · VERTU

OR

LES · PROSPÉRITÉ · DU · VICE

Firstly, that I have more memories in myself alone than all men have had since this world was a world.

Secondly, that the categores (flesh and word in the Scriptures) have not been read into the text but are announced in its voice directly.

Thirdly that the second explains why a Kiss stole a minute off of our lives

In fact we must break completely with the long-standing logical tradition based upon the unambiguous nature of identity and its legislation by the law of non-contradiction. However, this does not imply that the traditional-conceptual scheme is rendered effete, since in its rightful place orthodox logic remains central necessity. But it is incumbent upon us to see that with regard to the ultimate nature of things the central tautologies of accepted logic represent only half of the logical truth: the other half being represented by a non-static anti-identity logical order in the guise of an energetic state, which implies basic disruption of the central tautologies of accepted logic.

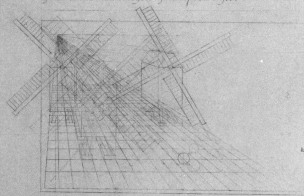

CLAUDIA HART

JUSTINE & JULIET, 1988
WOOD AND LEAVES, 23½ × 6½ × 27¼"
COURTESY PAT HEARN GALLERY, NEW YORK

CLAUDIA HART

BORN: 1955, NEW YORK CITY

MICHAEL HARDESTY

BORN: 1952, LOUISVILLE, KENTUCKY

MICHAEL HARDESTY

NIMBUS, 1988
INSTALLATION AT GERMANS VAN ECK GALLERY, NEW YORK, 1988
PLEXIGLAS, WOOD, NEON, SMOKE, VIDEO MONITOR
COURTESY GERMANS VAN ECK GALLERY, NEW YORK

STEVEN HEINO

BORN: 1952, SEATTLE, WASHINGTON

STEVEN HEINO
FIGURES OF SPEECH, 1985
MIXED MEDIA, 7 × 8'
STEVE CHASE COLLECTION, RANCHO MIRAGE, CALIFORNIA
COURTESY JAN BAUM GALLERY, LOS ANGELES

STEVEN HEINO
EFFIGY FIGURE, 1988
MIXED MEDIA AND LITHO PLATES ON WOOD, 79 × 29 × 8"
JAN BAUM GALLERY, LOS ANGELES

TISHAN HSU
BEING BLUE, 1986
OIL, ALKYD, ENAMEL, ACRYLIC, CEMENT COMPOUND ON WOOD, 60 × 60 × 4"
COURTESY PAT HEARN GALLERY, NEW YORK

TISHAN HSU

BORN: 1951, BOSTON, MASSACHUSETTS

TISHAN HSU

AUTOPSY, 1988
TILE, COMPOUND, CHROME, RUBBER, ACRYLIC, STEEL, WOOD, 55 × 49½ × 94"
COURTESY PAT HEARN GALLERY, NEW YORK

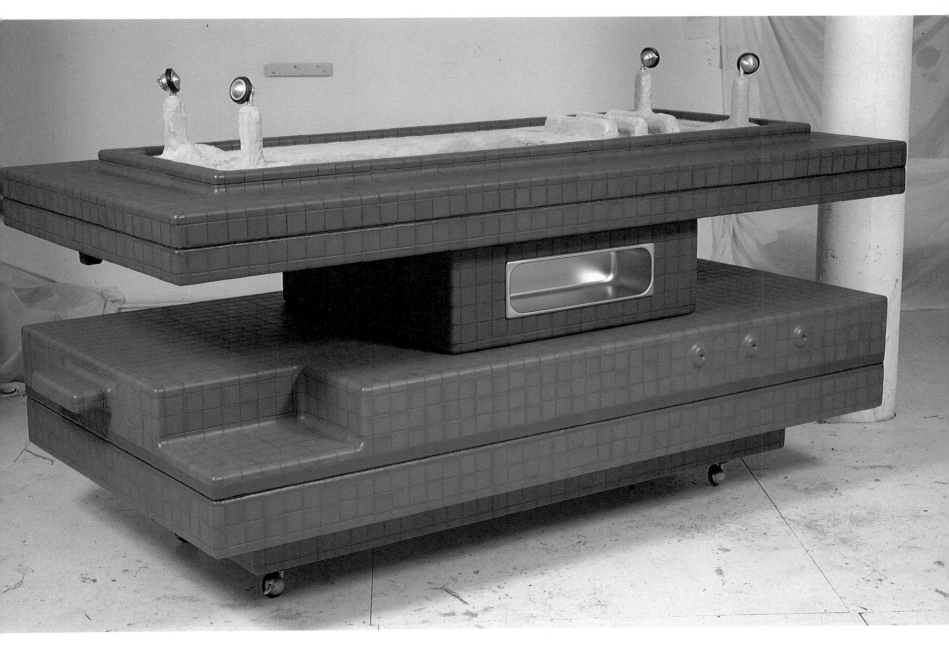

REBECCA HORN

BORN: 1944

REBECCA HORN

AN ART CIRCUS, 1988
INSTALLATION AT MARIAN GOODMAN GALLERY, NEW YORK, 1988
MUSEE DES BEAUX-ARTS, MONTREAL
COURTESY MARIAN GOODMAN GALLERY, NEW YORK

MARK INNERST
THE RESERVOIR (GREEN AND ROSE), 1987
OIL ON ACRYLIC ON BOARD, 10 × 20½"
PRIVATE COLLECTION
COURTESY CURT MARCUS GALLERY, NEW YORK

ALFREDO JAAR

BORN: 1966, SANTIAGO, CHILE

JIM ISERMANN
UNTITLED, 1989
ENAMEL PAINT, ORLON SHAG, AND WOOD, 96 × 96 × 2"
COURTESY FEATURE, NEW YORK

JIM ISERMANN
FUTURA, 1987
INSTALLATION AT LOS ANGELES COUNTY MUSEUM OF ART, 1987
COURTESY FEATURE, NEW YORK

JIM ISERMANN

BORN: 1955, KENOSHA, WISCONSIN

KRISTIN JONES AND ANDREW GINZEL
PANGAEA, 1985
FLAMES, VAPOR, SAND, WATER, LIGHT, $9 \times 12 \times 15'$

KRISTIN JONES AND ANDREW GINZEL

KRISTIN JONES
BORN: 1956, WASHINGTON, D.C.

ANDREW GINZEL
BORN: 1954, CHICAGO, ILLINOIS

ANISH KAPOOR
RED IN THE CENTER, 1982
BONDED EARTH AND PIGMENT, 10 × 13'
COURTESY BARBARA GLADSTONE GALLERY, NEW YORK

ANISH KAPOOR

BORN: 1954, BOMBAY, INDIA

ANISH KAPOOR
PLACE, 1985
MIXED MEDIA, 32 × 32 × 32"
COURTESY BARBARA GLADSTONE GALLERY, NEW YORK

BARBARA KASTEN

BORN: CALIFORNIA

JON KESSLER

BORN: 1957, YONKERS, NEW YORK

JON KESSLER

CRASHING BY DESIGN, 1986
MIXED-MEDIA CONSTRUCTION WITH LIGHTS AND MOTORS, 72½ × 47½ × 27½"
COURTESY LUHRING AUGUSTINE GALLERY, NEW YORK

BARBARA KASTEN

ARCHITECTURAL SITE 4, 1986
CIBACHROME PRINT, 47 × 60"
COURTESY JOHN WEBER GALLERY, NEW YORK

MIKE KELLEY
ANIMAL SELF AND *FRIENDS OF THE ANIMALS*, 1987
GLUED FELT, LEFT: 96 × 72"; RIGHT: 94¾ × 67¾"
COURTESY METRO PICTURES, NEW YORK

MIKE KELLEY

BORN: 1954, DETROIT, MICHIGAN

MIKE KELLEY
NO PLACE, 1989
GLUED FELT, SEWN, STUFFED CLOTH TOY, AND CORD, 100 × 127 × 6"
COURTESY METRO PICTURES, NEW YORK

JEFF KOONS
MICHAEL JACKSON & BUBBLES, 1988
PORCELAIN, 42 × 70½ × 32½"
COURTESY SONNABEND GALLERY, NEW YORK

JEFF KOONS

BORN: 1955, YORK, PENNSYLVANIA

JEFF KOONS

USHERING IN BANALITY, 1988
POLYCHROMED WOOD, EDITION OF THREE, 38 × 62 × 30"
COURTESY SONNABEND GALLERY, NEW YORK

IGOR KOPYSTIANSKI

BORN: 1954, LVOV, UKRAINIAN S.S.R.

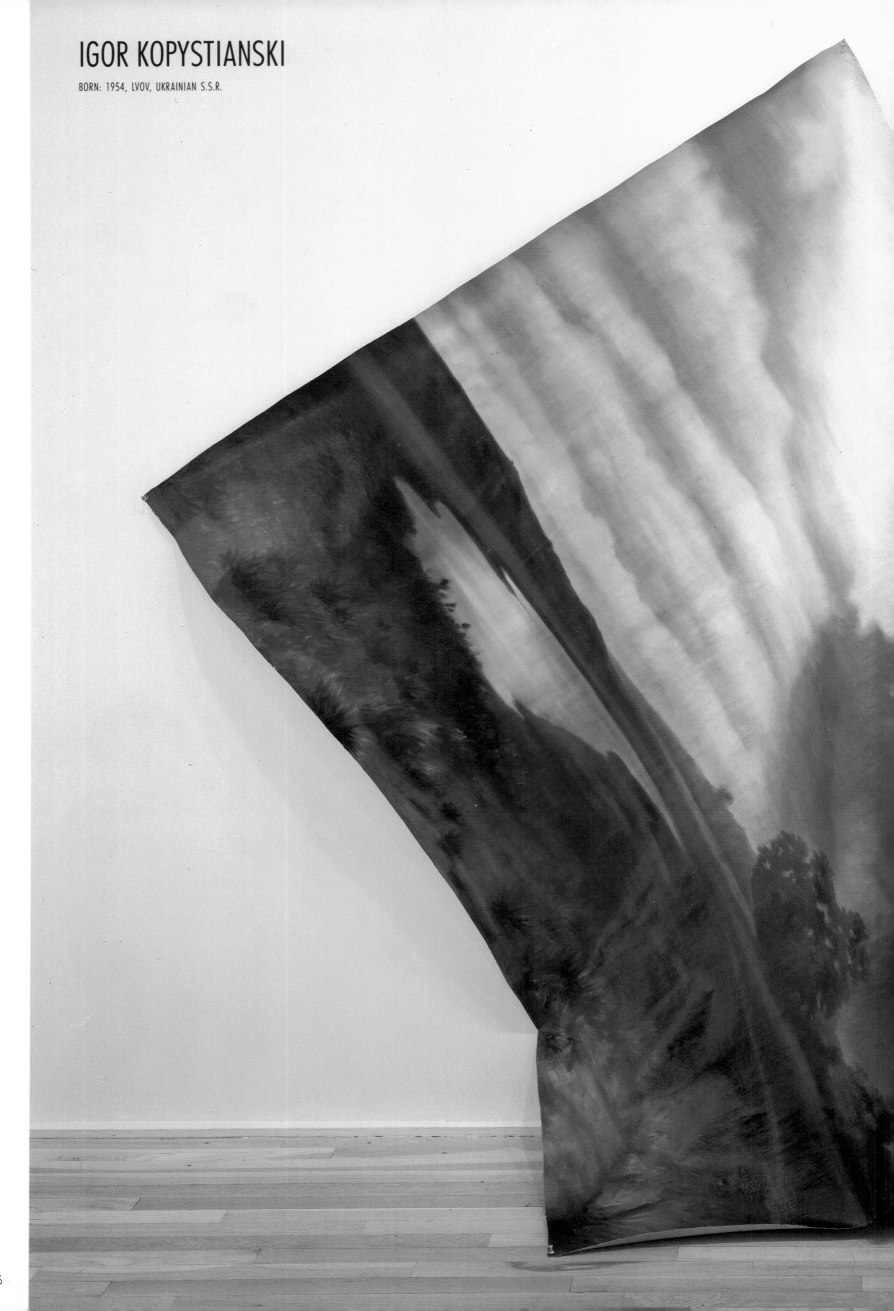

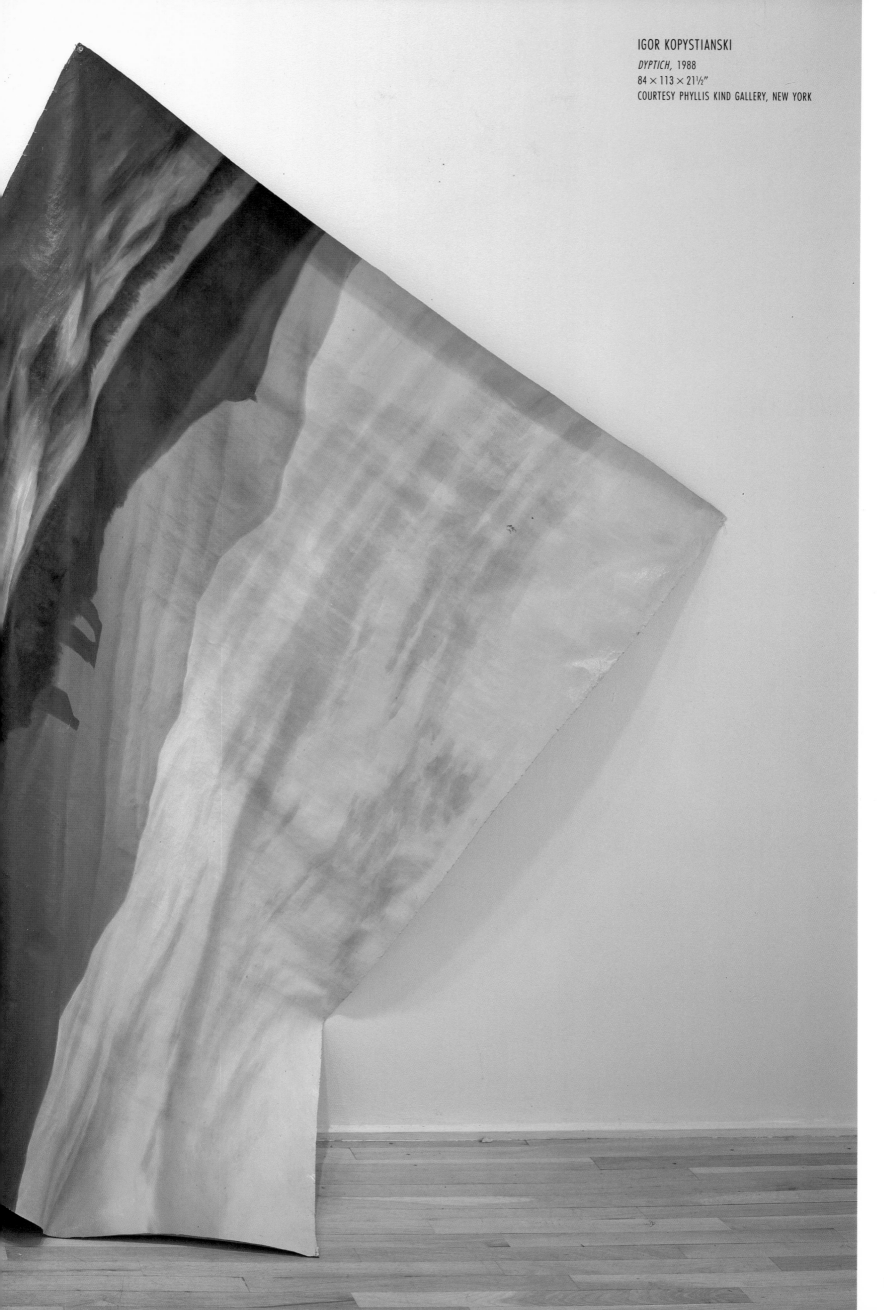

IGOR KOPYSTIANSKI
DYPTICH, 1988
84 × 113 × 21½"
COURTESY PHYLLIS KIND GALLERY, NEW YORK

WOLFGANG LAIB

BORN: 1950, METZINGER, WEST GERMANY

WOLFGANG LAIB
RICE HOUSE
INSTALLATION, 1988
MARBLE, RICE, AND HAZELNUT POLLEN, $7\frac{7}{8} \times 8\frac{5}{8} \times 50$"
COURTESY GALERIE LELONG, NEW YORK

LOUISE LAWLER

BORN: 1947, BRONXVILLE, NEW YORK

LOUISE LAWLER
THIS DRAWING IS FOR SALE, 1985
CIBACHROME PRINT (EDITION OF 5), 25½ × 38"
COURTESY METRO PICTURES, NEW YORK

JULIAN LETHBRIDGE
UNTITLED (CIRCLES), 1988
OIL ON LINEN, 48 × 36"
COURTESY PAULA COOPER GALLERY, NEW YORK

ANNETTE LEMIEUX

BORN: 1957, NORFOLK, VIRGINIA

ANNETTE LEMIEUX
THE GREAT OUTDOORS, 1989
LATEX ON CANVAS, LAMP, TABLE, AND CHAIR, 86½ × 142 × 48"
COLLECTION FREDERICH ROOS
COURTESY JOSH BAER GALLERY, NEW YORK

ERIK LEVINE
XXXXX, 1987
WOOD, 33 × 60 × 60"
COURTESY DIANE BROWN GALLERY, NEW YORK

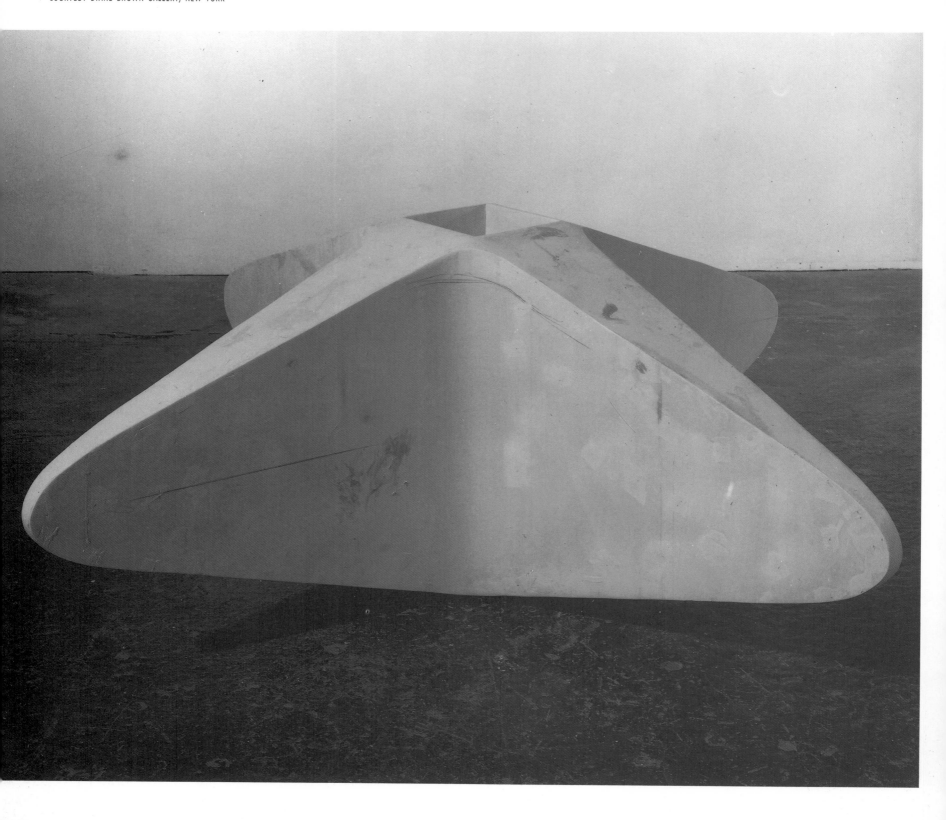

ERIK LEVINE

BORN: 1960, LOS ANGELES, CALIFORNIA

ERIK LEVINE

UNTITLED, 1989
PLYWOOD, $72 \times 77 \times 72$"
HIGH MUSEUM OF ART, ATLANTA
PURCHASE, WITH FUNDS FROM THE AWARDS IN THE VISUAL ARTS
AND THE 20TH CENTURY ART ACQUISITION FUND
COURTESY DIANE BROWN GALLERY, NEW YORK

ORLANDO GABINO LEYBA

BAYADERA, 1988
OIL ON CANVAS, 16 × 52"
COURTESY THE ARTIST

ORLANDO GABINO LEYBA

BORN: 1958, ESPANOLA, NEW MEXICO

ORLANDO GABINO LEYBA
ECHAR LUZ SOBRE MIS RAICES, 1988
OIL ON CANVAS, 48 × 56"
COURTESY THE ARTIST

DONALD LIPSKI

BORN: 1947, CHICAGO, ILLINOIS

DONALD LIPSKI
THE EAST, 1988
MOORING BUOY, COMPASSES, AND NAILS, DIAMETER: 5'
COURTESY GERMANS VAN ECK GALLERY, NEW YORK

THOMAS MACAULAY
INSTALLATION FOR WRIGHT STATE UNIVERSITY, 1985
PAPER, PAINT, PORTABLE WALLS, AND LADDERS, HEIGHT: 24'
COURTESY TWINING GALLERY, NEW YORK

THOMAS MACAULAY

BORN: NEW CARLISLE, OHIO

MCDERMOTT AND MCGOUGH

DAVID MCDERMOTT
BORN: 1952, HOLLYWOOD, CALIFORNIA
PETER MCGOUGH
BORN: 1958, SYRACUSE, NEW YORK

MCDERMOTT AND MCGOUGH
QUEER—1885, 1987
OIL AND GOLD LEAF ON LINEN, 44 × 88"
COURTESY MASSIMO AUDIELLO GALLERY, NEW YORK

MCDERMOTT AND MCGOUGH
SUMMER 1972, 1986
OIL ON CANVAS, 48 × 60"
COURTESY MASSIMO AUDIELLO GALLERY, NEW YORK

MCDERMOTT AND MCGOUGH
18TH-CENTURY SALON AS REFLECTED IN
A 19TH-CENTURY VASE, 1907, 1988
CYANOTYPE PRINT, 10 × 8"
COURTESY ROBERT MILLER GALLERY, NEW YORK

CHRIS MACDONALD

BORN: 1957, LYNN, MASSACHUSETTS

CHRIS MACDONALD
UNTITLED (TIE # II), 1988
WOOD, 6'10" × 4'3" × 18'1"
COURTESY DAVID BEITZEL GALLERY, NEW YORK

WALTER MARTIN

BORN: 1953, NORFOLK, VIRGINIA

WALTER MARTIN

SNAIL, SNAIL, COME OUT OF YOUR HOLE,
OR ELSE I'LL BEAT YOU BLACK AS A COAL, 1987
MIXED MEDIA, 61 × 128"
COURTESY P·P·O·W, NEW YORK

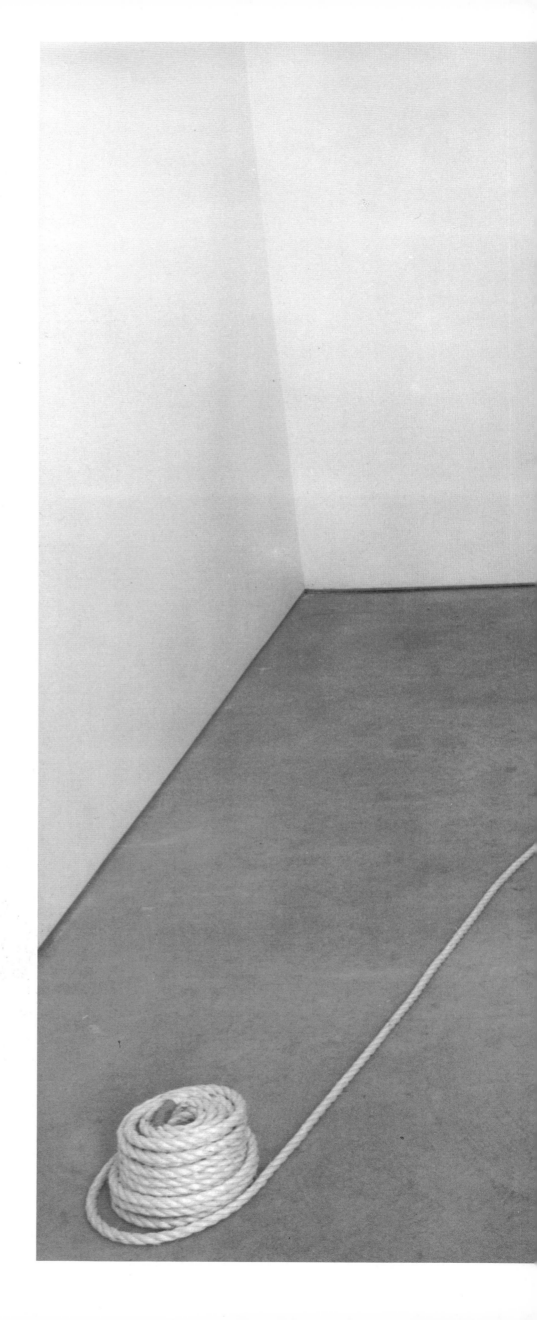

FRANK MAJORE

BORN: 1948, RICHMOND HILL, NEW YORK

FRANK MAJORE
VENUS
CIBACHROME PRINT, 24 × 20"
COURTESY HOLLY SOLOMON GALLERY, NEW YORK

ANDREW MENARD

FOLLY, 1988
FIBERGLASS, EPOXY RESIN, STYROFOAM,
POLYESTER RESIN, AND IRON POWDER, EACH: 84 × 34 × 18"
SCHULMAN SCULPTURE PARK, WESTCHESTER, NEW YORK
COURTESY BROOKE ALEXANDER GALLERY, NEW YORK

ANDREW MENARD

BORN: 1950, BOSTON, MASSACHUSETTS

MATT MULLICAN

BORN: 1951, SANTA MONICA, CALIFORNIA

MATT MULLICAN
UNTITLED (CITY), 1987
OIL STICK ON CANVAS
COURTESY MICHAEL KLEIN, INC., NEW YORK

MATT MULLICAN
UNTITLED, 1988
NYLON BANNERS, DOW JONES BUILDING, WORLD FINANCIAL CENTER,
NEW YORK COURTESY MICHAEL KLEIN, INC., NEW YORK

MARILYN MINTER

DOGS FROM HELL #3, 1988
ENAMEL ON CANVAS, 6 × 8′
COLLECTION W. S. B. FOUNDATION
COURTESY MAX PROTETCH GALLERY, NEW YORK

MARILYN MINTER

BORN: SHREVEPORT, LOUISIANA

JOYCE NEIMANAS

BORN: 1944, CHICAGO, ILLINOIS

JOYCE NEIMANAS

FEAST, 1987
SILVER GELATIN PRINT, 42 × 65½"
COURTESY THE ARTIST

JOYCE NEIMANAS
SUBLIME INSECURITY, 1988
SILVER GELATIN PRINT, 42 × 77"
DASHEIMER COLLECTION
COURTESY THE ARTIST

GERRY MOREHEAD

MAS CABESA, 1989
MIXED MEDIA ON WOOD, 48¼ × 96¼"
COURTESY MICHAEL KLEIN, INC., NEW YORK

GERRY MOREHEAD

BORN: 1949, COLUMBUS, OHIO

DAVID NELSON
MEASURED PAINTING, 1988
OIL ON WOOD PANELS, 36 × 108"
COURTESY THE ARTIST

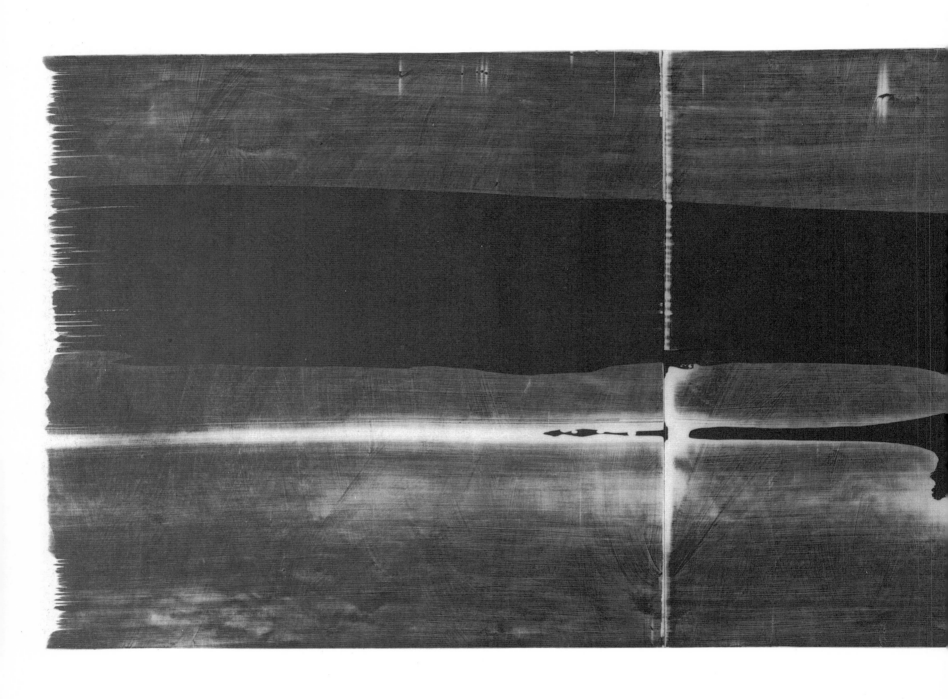

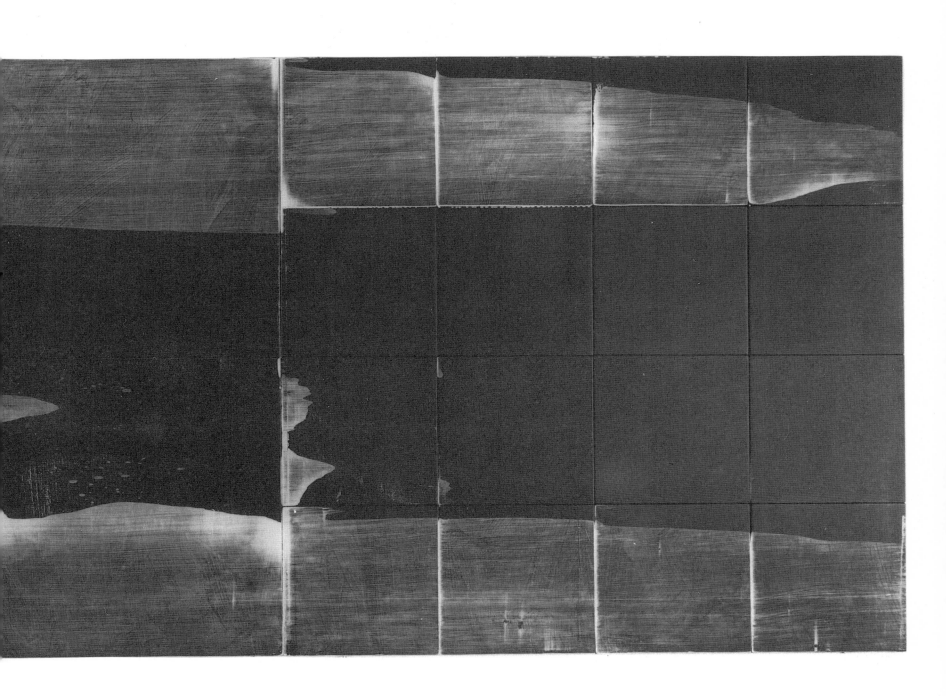

DAVID NELSON

BORN: 1960, RUNNING SPRINGS, CALIFORNIA

JOSEPH NECHVATAL
THE INFORMATION CULT'S PANOPTICONIC SUBJECT AS DECENTERED DATA, 1986
COMPUTER, ROBOTIC-ASSISTED, ACRYLIC ON CANVAS, 97½ × 139"
COURTESY BROOKE ALEXANDER GALLERY, NEW YORK

JOSEPH NECHVATAL

BORN: 1951, CHICAGO, ILLINOIS

PETER NAGY

VITA FUTURISTA, 1988
ACRYLIC ON CANVAS, 72 × 72"
COLLECTION MR. AND MRS. RICHARD RUBEN
COURTESY JAY GORNEY MODERN ART, NEW YORK

JOAN NELSON

BORN: 1958, TORRANCE, CALIFORNIA

JOAN NELSON
UNTITLED, 1988
OIL AND WAX ON WOOD, 21 × 16"
COURTESY ROBERT MILLER GALLERY, NEW YORK

DEBORAH OROPALLO
MINERS, 1989
OIL ON CANVAS, 110 × 18"
COURTESY STEPHEN WIRTZ GALLERY, SAN FRANCISCO

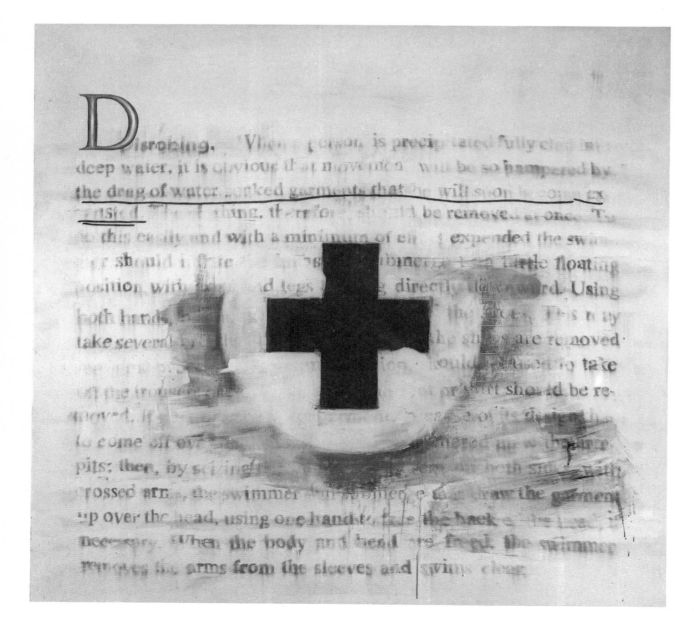

DEBORAH OROPALLO
WATER SAFETY, 1989
OIL ON CANVAS, 65 × 68"
COURTESY STEPHEN WIRTZ GALLERY, SAN FRANCISCO

 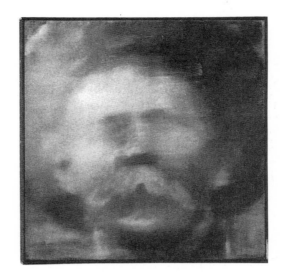 

DEBORAH OROPALLO

BORN: 1954, HACKENSACK, NEW JERSEY

JOEL OTTERSON

BORN: 1959, LOS ANGELES, CALIFORNIA

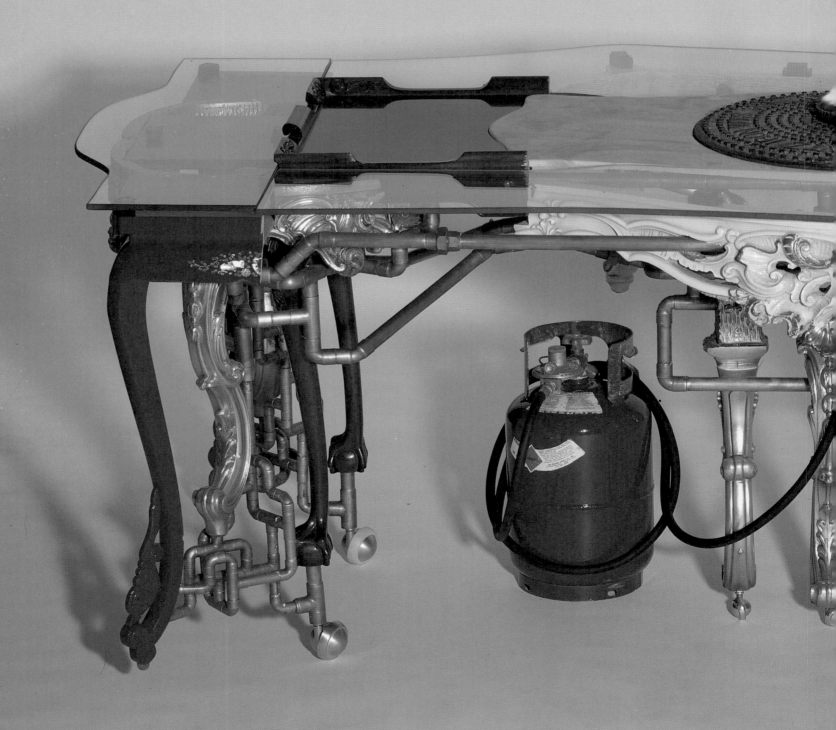

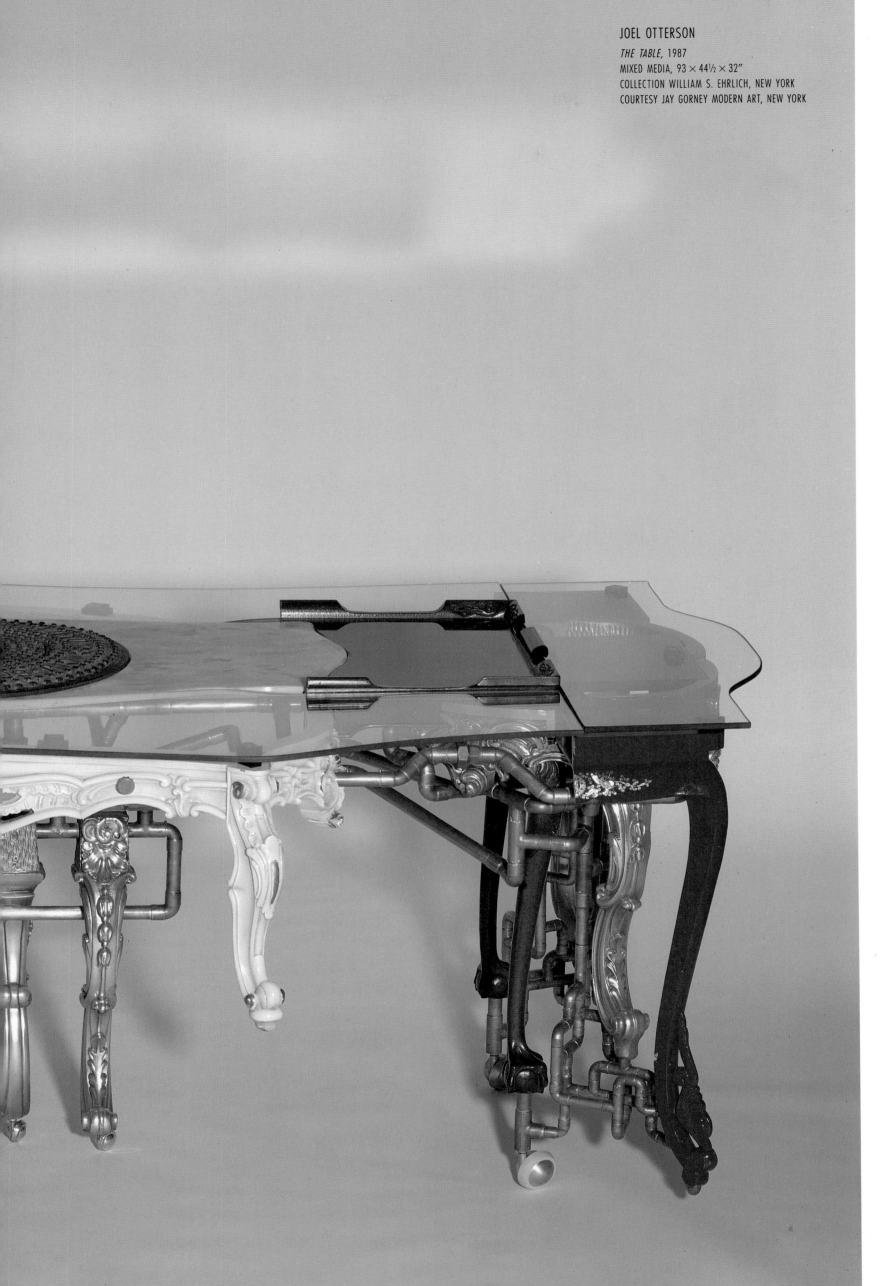

JOEL OTTERSON
THE TABLE, 1987
MIXED MEDIA, 93 × 44½ × 32"
COLLECTION WILLIAM S. EHRLICH, NEW YORK
COURTESY JAY GORNEY MODERN ART, NEW YORK

IZHAR PATKIN
WHITE GHOST (THE BLACK PAINTINGS), 1986
INK ON NEOPRENE, 14 × 28'
COLLECTION THE MUSEUM OF MODERN ART, NEW YORK
COURTESY HOLLY SOLOMON GALLERY, NEW YORK

IZHAR PATKIN

BORN: 1955, ISRAEL

IZHAR PATKIN
NIGHT AT THE BALAGANY, 1986
ENAMEL AND PAPER, 95 × 120"
COURTESY HOLLY SOLOMON GALLERY, NEW YORK

STEPHEN PRINA
INSTALLATION SHOT AT LUHRING AUGUSTINE GALLERY, 1988
COURTESY LUHRING AUGUSTINE GALLERY, NEW YORK

STEPHEN PRINA

BORN: 1954, GALESBURG, ILLINOIS

HOLT QUENTEL

BORN: 1961, MILWAUKEE, WISCONSIN

HOLT QUENTEL

WHITE 3 MESH AND STEEL POLES, 1988
LATEX, OIL, MESH, CANVAS, STEEL POLES, AND ROPE, 102 × 102"
SAATCHI COLLECTION, LONDON
COURTESY STUX GALLERY, NEW YORK

ELLEN PHELAN

BORN: 1943, DETROIT, MICHIGAN

RICHARD PRINCE

BORN: 1949, PANAMA CANAL ZONE

A traveling salesman's car broke down one evening on a lonely road and he asked at the only farm house in sight. "Can you put me up for the nite?" "I reckon I can," said the farmer. "But you'll have to share the room with my young son ." "How about that!" gasped the salesman. "I'm in the wrong joke."

CHARLES RAY
HOW A TABLE WORKS, 1986
MIXED MEDIA, 44½ × 46 × 32"
COLLECTION LANNAN FOUNDATION, LOS ANGELES
COURTESY FEATURE, NEW YORK

CHARLES RAY

BORN: 1953, CHICAGO, ILLINOIS

TIM ROLLINS & K.O.S.

TIM ROLLINS
BORN: 1955, PITTSFIELD, MAINE

K.O.S

ARACELIS BATISTA
BORN: 1974, NEW YORK CITY

BRENDA CARLO
BORN: 1974, NEW YORK CITY

RICHARD CRUZ
BORN: 1970, NEW YORK CITY

GEORGE GARCES
BORN: 1972, NEW YORK CITY

CHRISTOPHER HERNANDEZ
BORN: 1978, NEW YORK CITY

NELSON MONTES
BORN: 1972, NEW YORK CITY

JOSE PARISSI
BORN: 1968, PONCE, PUERTO RICO

CARLOS RIVERA
BORN: 1971, NEW YORK CITY

ANNETTE ROSADO
BORN: 1972, NEW YORK CITY

NELSON SAVINON
BORN: 1972, NEW YORK CITY

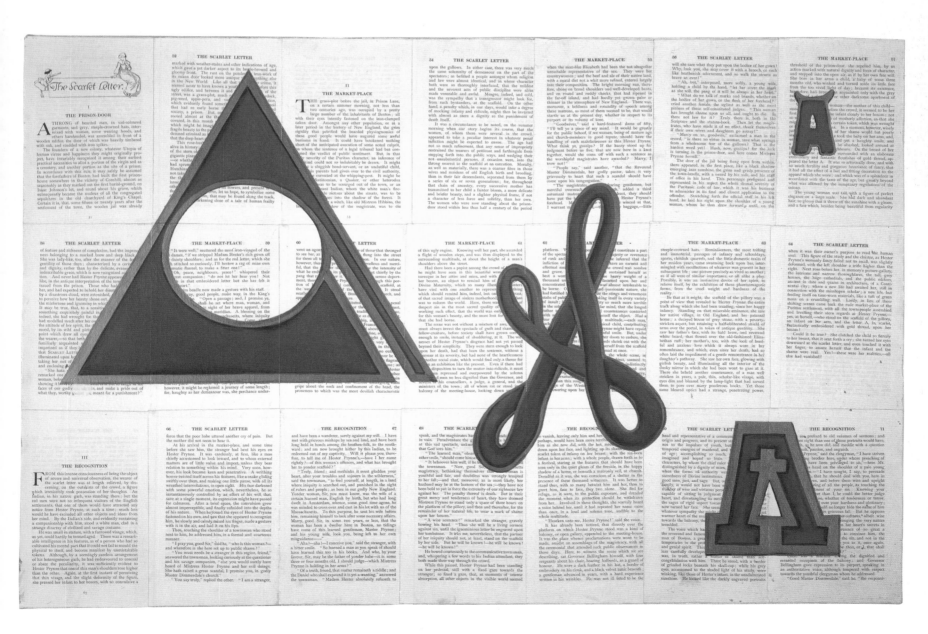

TIM ROLLINS & K.O.S.
STUDY FOR THE SCARLET LETTER I, 1987–88
ACRYLIC, WATERCOLOR, AND BISTRE ON BOOKPAGES ON LINEN, 24 × 36"
COLLECTION MR. AND MRS. KEITH SACHS
COURTESY JAY GORNEY MODERN ART, NEW YORK

MARTHA ROSLER

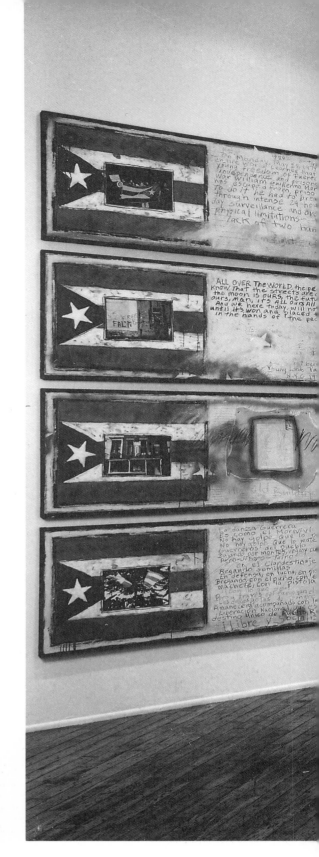

MARTHA ROSLER
HOME FRONT
INSTALLATION AT DIA ART FOUNDATION, NEW YORK, 1989
COURTESY DIA ART FOUNDATION, NEW YORK

LOUIS SCIULLO

BORN: 1958, PITTSBURGH, PENNSYLVANIA

LOUIS SCIULLO
PROOFS ON (EX)ISTENCE: 9TH PROOF: MESSENGERS, 1988
OIL ON PANEL, 24 × 24 × 4"
COURTESY GRACIE MANSION GALLERY

ANDRES SERRANO
MILK, BLOOD, 1987
CIBACHROME PRINT, 40 × 60"
COURTESY STUX GALLERY, NEW YORK

ANDRES SERRANO

BORN: 1950, NEW YORK CITY

LAURIE SIMMONS
TOURISM: THE PARTHENON, 1984
COLOR PHOTOGRAPH, 40 × 60"
COURTESY METRO PICTURES, NEW YORK

RAY SMITH
MARIA DE LA CRUZ COMO CHOC-MOOL, 1988
OIL ON WOOD, 96 × 192"
PRIVATE COLLECTION
COURTESY SPERONE WESTWATER GALLERY, NEW YORK

RAY SMITH

BORN: 1959, BROWNSVILLE, TEXAS

RAY SMITH
LUCHA POLITICA, 1988
OIL ON WOOD, 84 × 144"
COLLECTION MARTIN SKLAR, NEW YORK
COURTESY SPERONE WESTWATER GALLERY, NEW YORK

KEN SOFER

BORN: 1953, NEW YORK CITY

KEN SOFER
WABASH, 1988
OIL ON STEEL ON WOOD, 48 × 42"
PRIVATE COLLECTION, ATLANTA
COURTESY M-13 GALLERY, NEW YORK

HAIM STEINBACH

BORN: 1944, ISRAEL

HAIM STEINBACH
SPIRIT I, 1987
MIXED-MEDIA CONSTRUCTION, 83 × 96 × 91"
MUSEE D'ART CONTEMPORAIN, BORDEAUX
COURTESY SONNABEND GALLERY AND
JAY GORNEY MODERN ART, NEW YORK

SUSAN SOLANO

BORN: 1946, BARCELONA, SPAIN

SUSAN SOLANO

ESTACIO TERMAL NO. 2, 1987
GALVANIZED IRON, 45¼ × 83¾ × 114¼"
COURTESY JACK SHAINMAN GALLERY, NEW YORK

STARN TWINS (DOUG AND MIKE)
FILM TUNNEL WITH MAN, 1987–88
TONED SILVER PRINT AND ORTHO FILM,
TAPE, GLUE, AND WOOD, 106 × 216"
COURTESY STUX GALLERY, NEW YORK

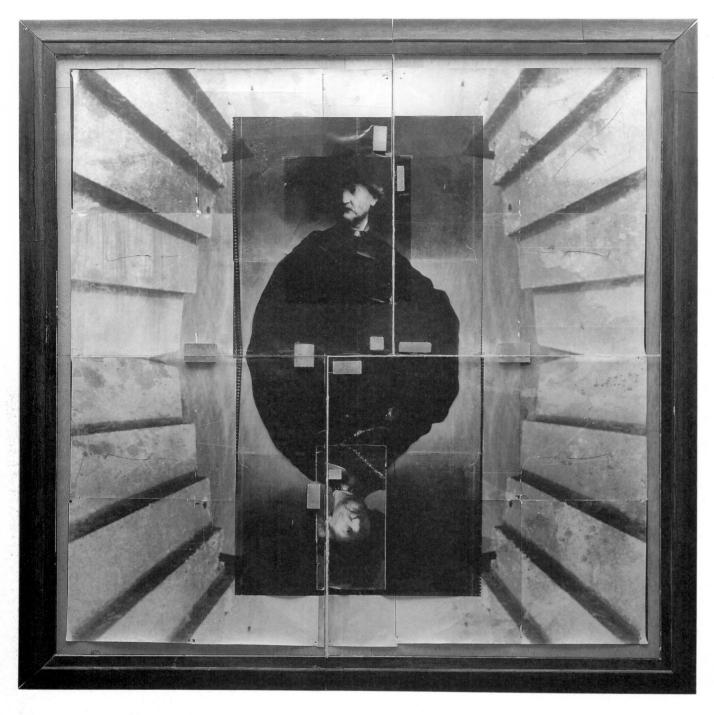

STARN TWINS (DOUG AND MIKE)
DOUBLE REMBRANDT WITH STEPS, 1987–88
TONED SILVER PRINT AND TONED ORTHO FILM, GLUE, PLEXIGLAS, AND WOOD, 108 × 108"
COLLECTION THE ARTISTS
COURTESY STUX GALLERY AND LEO CASTELLI, NEW YORK

STARN TWINS (MIKE AND DOUG)

BORN: 1961

ROSEMARIE TROCKEL

BORN: 1952, SCHWERTZ, WEST GERMANY

ROSEMARIE TROCKEL
UNTITLED, 1988
WOOD, MASONITE, GLASS, FOAM RUBBER, CARDBOARD,
PLASTER, AND SILVER BRACELET, 70½ × 63 × 27½"
COURTESY BARBARA GLADSTONE GALLERY, NEW YORK

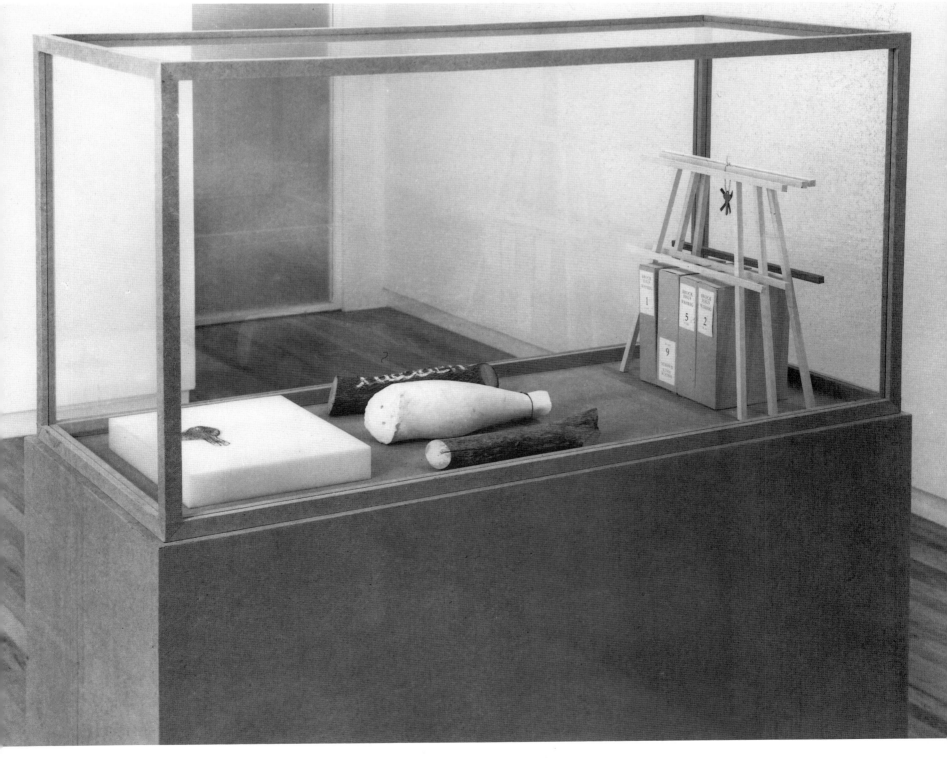

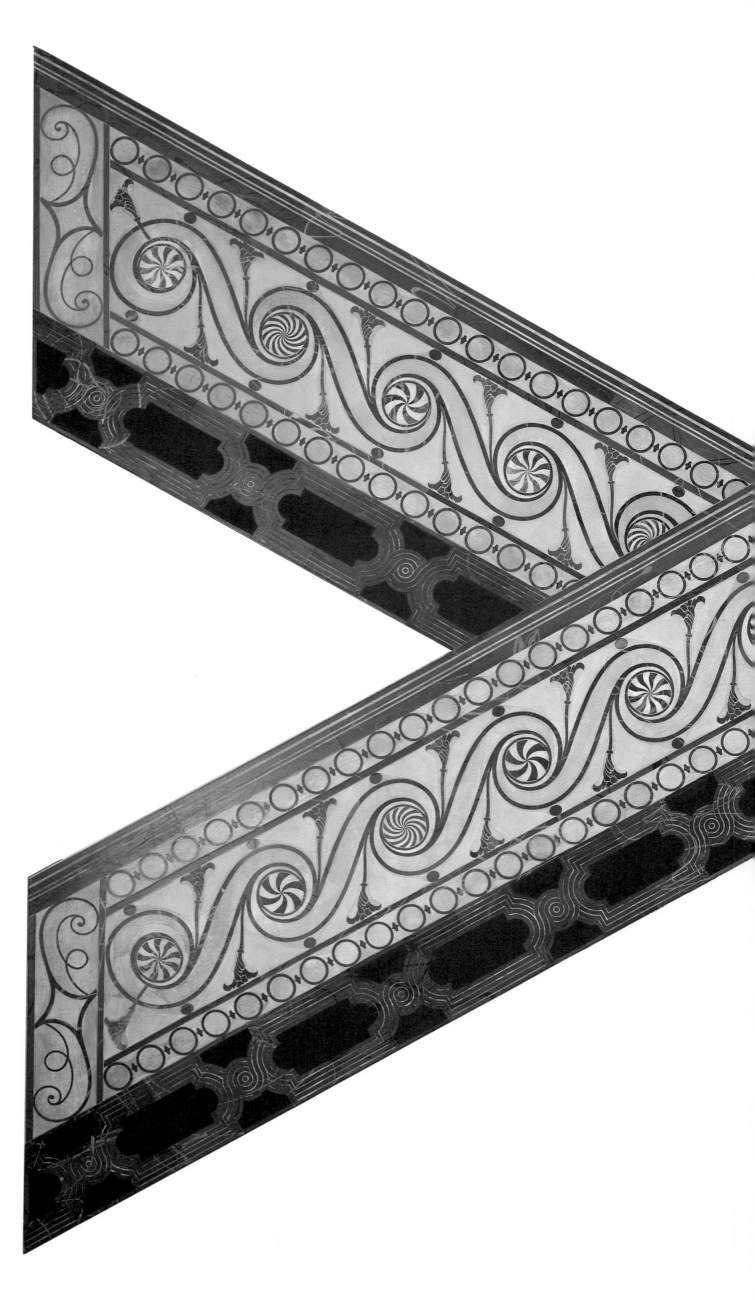

PHILIP TAAFFE

BORN: 1955, ELIZABETH, NEW JERSEY

PHILIP TAAFFE
INTERSECTING BALUSTRADES, 1987
ENAMEL, SILKSCREEN COLLAGE, AND ACRYLIC ON CANVAS, 130 × 156"
COURTESY PAT HEARN GALLERY, NEW YORK

WILLIAM STONE

BORN: 1944, NEW JERSEY

WILLIAM STONE

CORRECT TIME, 1987
CLOCK AND QUARTZ APPARATUS, 14 × 18 × 4½"
COURTESY TOM CUGLIANI GALLERY, NEW YORK

WILLIAM STONE

IN DREAMS BEGIN RESPONSIBILITIES, 1988
OAK, PLYWOOD, BRASS HEAD AND FOOTBOARDS, AND CARPET, 94 × 44 × 72"
COURTESY TOM CUGLIANI GALLERY, NEW YORK

MIERLE LADERMAN UKELES
CEREMONIAL ARCH HONORING SERVICE WORKERS IN THE NEW SERVICE ECONOMY, 1988
STEEL ARCH WITH MATERIALS DONATED FROM CITY AGENCIES, 11' × 12'4" × 9'
COURTESY RONALD FELDMAN FINE ARTS, NEW YORK

MIERLE LADERMAN UKELES

BORN: 1939, COLORADO

MIERLE LADERMAN UKELES
CEREMONIAL ARCH HONORING SERVICE WORKERS IN THE NEW SERVICE ECONOMY (DETAIL), 1988

MEYER VAISMAN
THE LEFT BEHIND, 1987
PROCESS INKS ON CANVAS, 98 × 209 × 10"
COURTESY SONNABEND GALLERY AND JAY GORNEY MODERN ART, NEW YORK

MEYER VAISMAN

BORN: 1960, CARACAS, VENEZUELA

MEYER VAISMAN
THE LEFT BEHIND, 1987
PROCESS INKS ON CANVAS, 45 × 37 × 7"
COLLECTION THOMAS AMMANN
COURTESY SONNABEND GALLERY AND JAY GORNEY MODERN ART, NEW YORK

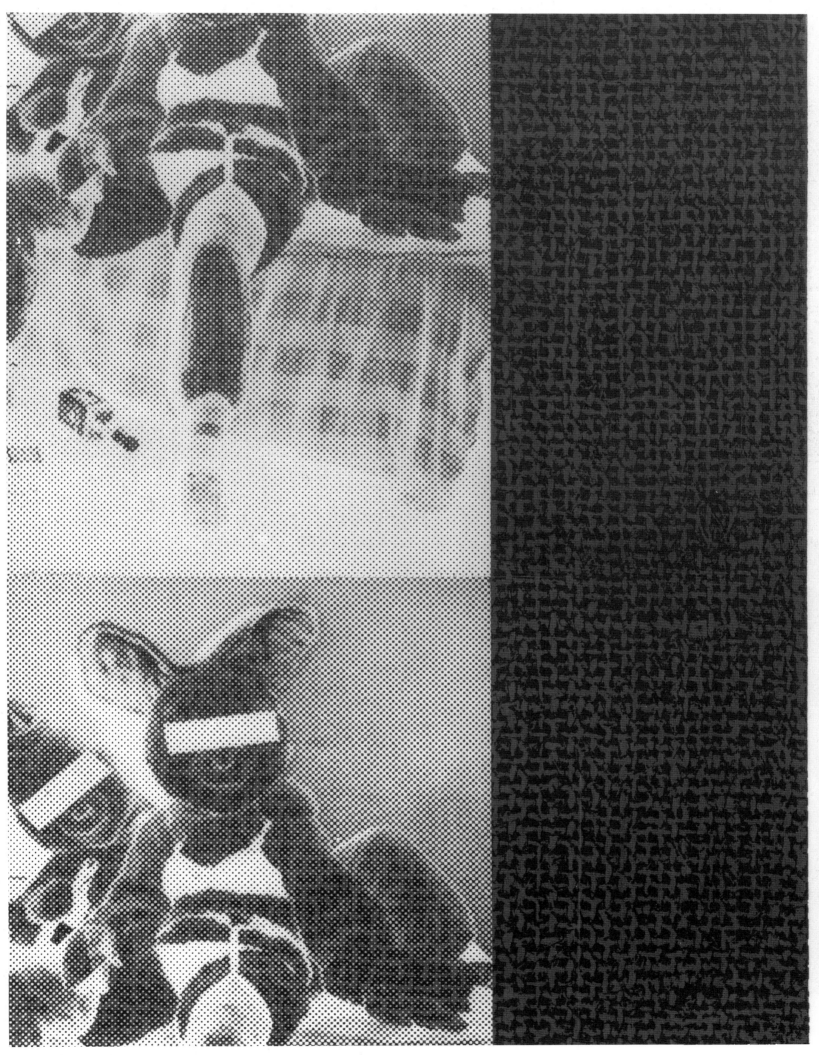

BILL VIOLA

BORN: 1951, NEW YORK CITY

BILL VIOLA
THE SLEEP OF REASON, 1988
VIDEO/SOUND INSTALLATION
THE CARNEGIE MUSEUM OF ART, PITTSBURGH. GIFT OF MILTON FINE
AND GIFT FUND FOR SPECIFIC ACQUISITIONS, 1988

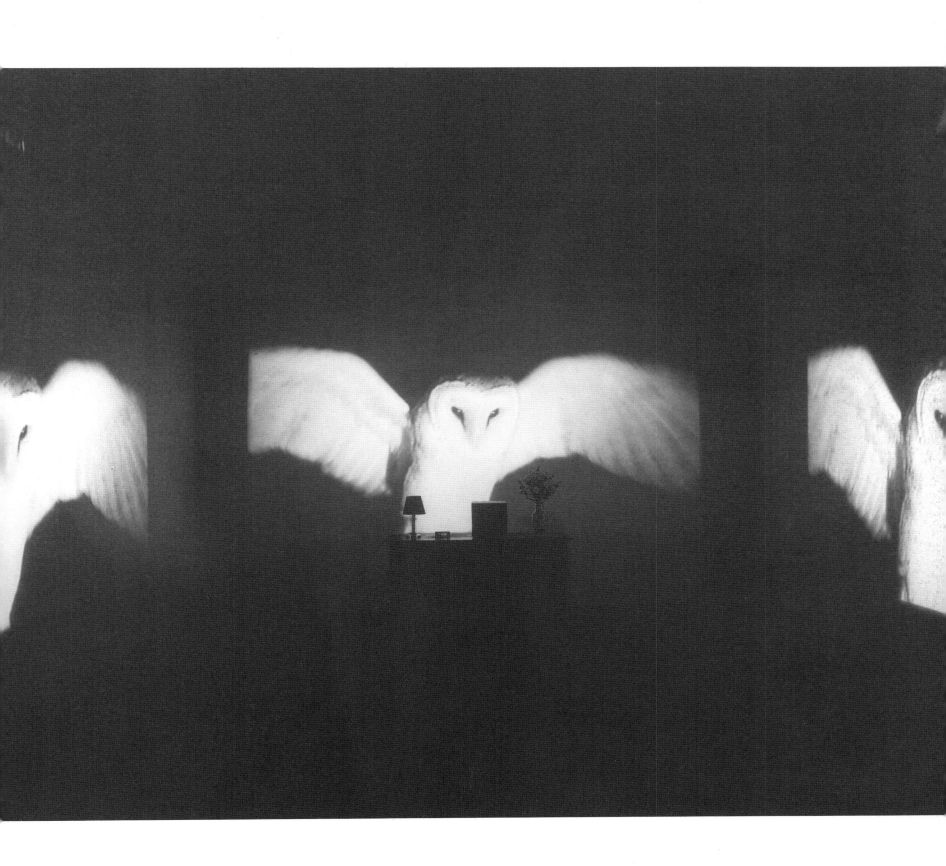

BOYD WEBB

BORN: 1947, CHRISTCHURCH, NEW ZEALAND

BOYD WEBB
THAW, 1989
UNIQUE CIBACHROME, 48 × 62″
COURTESY SONNABEND GALLERY, NEW YORK

MEG WEBSTER

BORN: 1944, SAN FRANCISCO, CALIFORNIA

MEG WEBSTER

HOLLOW, 1984–85
PACKED EARTH AND PERENNIALS, 25 × 90'
NASSAU COUNTY MUSEUM OF ART, ROSLYN, NEW YORK
COURTESY BARBARA GLADSTONE GALLERY, NEW YORK

MEG WEBSTER

GLEN, 1988
EARTH, STEEL, PLANTS, AND FIELDSTONE, MINNEAPOLIS SCULPTURE GARDEN
COURTESY WALKER ART CENTER AND BARBARA GLADSTONE GALLERY, NEW YORK

NEIL WINOKUR

BORN: 1945, NEW YORK CITY

NEIL WINOKUR
ROBERT ROSENBLUM, 1987
FIVE CIBACHROME PRINTS (FRAMED AND INSTALLED), 41¾ × 69"
COURTESY BARBARA TOLL FINE ARTS, NEW YORK

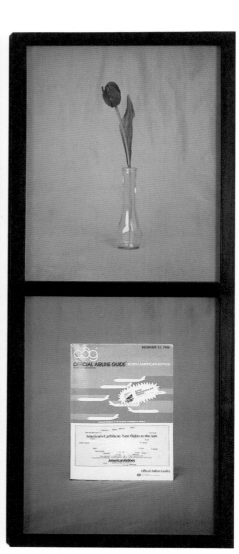

ROBIN WINTERS
EVERLASTING LIGHT, 1987
ACRYLIC ON CANVAS, 41 × 70"
COURTESY MICHAEL KLEIN, INC., NEW YORK

ROBIN WINTERS

BORN: 1950, BENICIA, CALIFORNIA

CHRISTOPHER WOOL
UNTITLED, 1988
ALKYD AND FLASHE ON ALUMINUM, 96 × 72"
COURTESY LUHRING AUGUSTINE GALLERY, NEW YORK

CHRISTOPHER WOOL

APOCALYPSE NOW, 1988
ALKYD AND FLASHE ON ALUMINUM AND STEEL, 84 × 72"
COURTESY LUHRING AUGUSTINE GALLERY, NEW YORK

BILL WOODROW

BORN: 1948, ENGLAND

BILL WOODROW

STILL WATERS, 1985
THREE CAR HOODS, THREE BOX SPRINGS, ENAMEL AND
ACRYLIC PAINTS, 54 × 122 × 245"
LA JOLLA MUSEUM OF ART, LA JOLLA, CALIFORNIA
COURTESY BARBARA GLADSTONE GALLERY, NEW YORK

MICHELE ZALOPANY

UNTITLED (CHILDREN), 1988
CHARCOAL AND PASTEL ON PAPER MOUNTED ON CANVAS, 60½ × 48½"
COURTESY MASSIMO AUDIELLO GALLERY, NEW YORK

MICHELE ZALOPANY

UNTITLED (GARDEN), 1988
CHARCOAL AND PASTEL ON PAPER MOUNTED ON CANVAS, 84¾ × 60½"
COURTESY MASSIMO AUDIELLO GALLERY, NEW YORK

TOM WUDL

BORN: 1948, COCHABAMBA, BOLIVIA

TOM WUDL
*THE BIRTH OF JAN VAN EYCK AND THE EXTENT OF HIS INFLUENCE
ON THE ART OF PAINTING, FOR A PERIOD OF 600 YEARS,* 1988
OIL ON CANVAS, 96 × 60"
ED BROIDA COLLECTION, LOS ANGELES
COURTESY L.A. LOUVER GALLERY, VENICE, CALIFORNIA

MICHAEL ZWACK

BORN: 1949, BUFFALO, NEW YORK

MICHAEL ZWACK
HISTORY OF THE WORLD, 1988
RAW PIGMENT AND OIL ON PAPER, 80 × 108"
PRIVATE COLLECTION
COURTESY CURT MARCUS GALLERY, NEW YORK

PHOTOGRAPH CREDITS

DATE DUE